6012

£10

Deborah

THE BOOK OF
THE SIAMESE CAT

I. Hillcross Fidelia, a very handsome female with beautiful light coat and good eye colour. Owner, Mrs. E. Towe. Breeder, Mrs. Gunn.

The Book of

THE
SIAMESE
CAT

by Rose Tenent

ROCKLIFF

SALISBURY SQUARE
LONDON

MADE AND PRINTED IN GREAT BRITAIN BY
THE CAMELOT PRESS LTD., LONDON AND SOUTHAMPTON

Acknowledgments

THE Author expresses her thanks to the many people who have kindly supplied illustrations and material for this book, in particular Mr. Michael Joseph for permission to quote from *Charles*, Mr. and Mrs. James Mason and Messrs. Michael Joseph Ltd. for the extract from *The Cats in Our Lives*, and Mr. Beverley Nichols, Miss Olivia Manning, Miss Pamela Wynne and Miss Vivien Leigh for their personal assistance with Chapter 10. Thanks are also due to Mrs. K. R. Williams for her notes and sketch of the Stud House in Chapter 5, to Miss Hettie Gray Baker of New York City for material included in Chapter 11, and to Mr. Albert A. Steward of the Cats Protection League for the loan of books from his personal library.

Contents

Illustrations

ix

Illustrations

I

History of the Breed

POPULAR as Siamese cats are to-day, until sixty or seventy years ago few people in the West had even seen one. Indeed, in the late Harrison Weir's book, *Our Cats and All About Them*, published during the latter part of the nineteenth century, he told how Crystal Palace catalogues recorded that up to the year 1887 there were only fifteen females and four males on show.

But this is not surprising as it may at first appear, because for generations these Royal cats were guarded jealously by the King of Siam in his Palace at Bangkok. It was almost impossible for a male to be smuggled out, as strict orders were given for all to be made neuter.

So deeply did the Royal household feel about their pets that they believed them to be sacred and thought that they enshrined the spirits of the dead. When any of the Royal princes was buried, a favourite cat would be entombed alive with him, the idea being that if it managed to escape through one of the small holes in the roof of the

I

burying-place, then the priests would know that the dead man's soul had passed into the cat's body.

These Palace or temple cats were said to be dark-coated, with golden eyes, while two distinct markings on the back distinguished them from the more common blue-eyed variety. There is an old superstition in Siam about these cats which makes many people want to own both types. It says that a blue-eyed cat represents silver and a yellow-eyed cat stands for gold. Therefore he who owns one of each will never want for anything.

It is probably owing to the early confinement of the Siamese cat that so very little is known of its origins. One school of thought says that it is a direct descendant of the ancient Egyptian cat, being the result of inter-mating when the Egyptian merchants took their pets on business travels in the Far East. Another opinion has it that the Siamese cat was originally bred from an albino, a freak cat which was probably given to the King of Siam owing to its exceptional rarity.

Yet a third belief states that the Siamese cat is the result of cross-mating between the sacred cat of Burma and the Annamese cat, the latter being imported into Siam about three centuries ago at the time of the great victory of the Siamese and Annamese peoples over the Cambodian Empire of the Kymers. The sacred cat of Burma, according to Russell Gordon, was much like the Siamese cat in colouring, but had long hair, a bushy tail, and white toes on all four feet. Judging by the white toes we still occasionally see on third-rate specimens of Siamese cats, I am of the opinion that this last theory may be the correct one.

Whatever the true starting-point, eventually a pair of

Siamese cats was brought to Britain in 1884 and shown to the public at Crystal Palace in the following year. These first specimens were brought over by Mr. Owen Gould, who was then Consul-General at Bangkok. Afterwards he presented them to his sister, Mrs. Veley, who subsequently became one of the first members of the Siamese Cat Club when it was founded in 1901.

During 1886 another pair of Siamese cats and two kittens were imported into Britain, this time by a Mrs. Vyvyan, who, in a letter to the late Harrison Weir, had the following comments to make on her pets:

"They are very affectionate and personally attached to their human friends, not liking to be left alone, and following us from room to room more after the manner of dogs than cats.

" 'Saiwan' is very clever at undoing the latch of the window in order to let himself out; tying it up with string is of no use, and he has even managed to untwist wire that has been used to prevent his going out in the snow."

By this time fanciers were beginning to take an immense interest in these very unusual cats. For the most part, the early specimens were of a grey or light dun colour, with well-marked muzzle, ears, legs, and tail all of a very dark chocolate brown. Their eyes were described as being a beautiful blue by day, and of a red colour at night. They had amusing, kinky tails.

There are many legends concerning the kinked tail. One of them says it originated through a Siamese princess who was frightened of losing her rings while she bathed in a stream. Looking round her for somewhere convenient to

3

place the jewellery, she noticed that her favourite cat had crooked his tail for her benefit. And since that time all Siamese cats have been born with a tiny kink at the end of their tails!

Another legend tells amusingly how a young cat took his wife into the jungle to search for a royal goblet that was missing from one of the Siamese temples. Upon finding the treasure, they decided that the female should remain in the jungle to guard it while the male went back to the city to inform the priest of their discovery. So the little cat took up her position among the leaves and tangled foliage, her tail twisted round the stem of the goblet to make quite sure that no one would try to take it away. Four nights later her husband returned to find he was the father of five sweet little kittens. But, in spite of her new responsibility, the loyal mother cat had not forgotten her earlier trust. Indeed, so conscientious had she been in her protection of the goblet that a permanent kink had developed in the end of her tail. What was more, all five kittens had a similar kink in their tails!

So much for legend. A far more probable theory, and one I think that many breeders adhere to, is that the kinked tail is the result of crosses between the Siamese and the Malayan cat or the sacred cat of Burma. Both these types were noted for kinked and knotted tails. Again, this feature could easily be a consequence of inbreeding at the Palace of Bangkok.

But characteristic as it was of the early specimens, the kinked tail is certainly not an asset to the Siamese of the present day. This is not to say that a tiny kink at the tip of a cat's tail would spoil its chances at a show if other physical qualities came up to the required standard. Indeed, many authorities on the breed regret the passing of this eminent feature. Among these is the distinguished judge and breeder, Mrs. Duncan Hindley, who has often expressed her feelings on this matter. Yet another great admirer of the kinked tail is the famous novelist, Compton Mackenzie, who is also President of the Siamese Cat Club. On more than one occasion of the annual Championship Show he has raised the subject, saying how sorry he is that the kinked tail is no longer an advantage.

This brings us to the important question as to what is the required standard of the present-day Siamese cat? Of the three types in existence, the seal-pointed variety is at present the most abundant and probably the most popular. This cat should be medium in size, with long, agile body, slim legs, and oval-shaped paws. The hind legs are always slightly longer than the front ones, and the tail of a really good specimen is long, thin, and tapering like a whip.

The seal-pointed Siamese is cream in colour, and this shades gradually into a pale warm fawn on the back. The quality of the coat should be even—that is, very short and fine in texture, glossy and close-lying. With the exception of very tiny kittens, the points—which are mask, ears, legs, feet, and tail—are all a dense and clearly defined seal brown; kittens are born quite white.

In definite contrast to our own round-faced British cats, the Siamese has a long head, and, to quote the official standard of points drawn up by the Siamese Cat Club, it should be "well proportioned, with width between the eyes, narrowing in perfectly straight lines to a fine muzzle, giving

5

the impression of a marten face. Ears, rather large and pricked, wide at the base".

To obtain a good idea of what such a cat should look like, turn to the photograph of Champion Inwood Shadow, who, up to the time of writing, has been widely acclaimed as the best Siamese female seen in Britain since the war. Quite apart from the "points" that are evident from her picture, Shadow has a beautiful pale coat and very expressive blue eyes. She is holder of four championships, twenty-three firsts and many other awards. At the National Cat Club's Championship Show in 1949 she was easily voted best exhibit. In fact, several judges have described this lovely cat as almost impossible to fault.

But perhaps what strikes one most about a Siamese cat on first acquaintance is the wonderful colour of its eyes, which in the best specimens is sapphire blue. The shape should be Oriental and slanting towards the nose. Many an admirer has bought a kitten for the beauty and expression of its eyes, and when the American film star, Mary Astor, wrote her book on Siamese cats, she called it *My Friends have Blue Eyes*.

And please do not imagine that all Siamese cats squint. Indeed, it was not until a pair called Pho and Mia were brought into this country, some fifteen years after the first immigrants, that the defect was even noticed. It is true the tendency does persist in some kittens, but with a really good specimen no squint should be apparent.

Answering to all the same rules regarding shape, size and character is the blue-pointed Siamese, which, as the name implies, has blue-grey points in place of the more familiar dark brown ones. Originally regarded as a "sport", at one

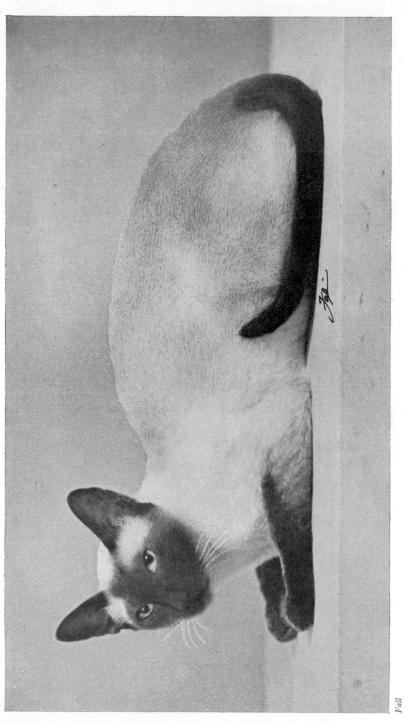

Fall

II. Champion Inwood Shadow (see pages 6 and 98).

III, IV. Chocolate-pointed kittens, exhibited by Mrs. K. R. Williams, at the Southern Counties Cat Club's Championship Show, January, 1950. This was the first entire litter of Chocolate-points to be bred and exhibited in Britain, probably in the world.

V, VI. Silbe Selene (Blue-pointed Siamese) and George (Seal-pointed Siamese) owned by Mrs. E. Silten of Mill Hill, London.

VII.   Bé-Bé, Blue-pointed Queen belonging to Mrs. E. Pinder of Mundesley, Norfolk.

VIII.   Mrs. F. Macdonald's "Raard" Blue-pointed Siamese Kittens.

time it was the opinion of most experts that there would never be a great demand for these little cats. It is interesting to recall the late Phyl Wade's remarks on the subject. Mrs. Wade was Chairman of the Siamese Cat Club, and this is what she wrote in her book, *The Siamese Cat*, published by Methuen & Co. Ltd. in 1934:

"Very few people outside the cat fancy have seen a blue-pointed Siamese. These can be most beautiful, with their blue instead of seal-brown points, and a bluey tinge of the coat. They are apparently 'sports', for no one quite knows how they come and one cannot definitely breed them. Certain studs sometimes throw them, although there may be nothing in their pedigree to account for this."

Several enthusiastic breeders, however, were quite convinced that it was possible to breed them, and determined that one day this attractive variety would be registered on its own. Not only has this come to pass but there is now a flourishing club run entirely for blue-points. Also, it was Champion Pincop Azure Kym, a lovely blue-point owned by a breeder in the Midlands, who won the coveted award of "Best in Show" at the Siamese Cat Club's Championship Show in 1948.

Although research has proved that the history of the chocolate-pointed Siamese in Britain dates back to an imported cat in 1896, little was known of this variety until fairly recently. Certain breeders have always been enthusiastic, and although separate classes at the Siamese Cat Club's Show were assigned to chocolate-points in 1948, until May 1950 they were still entered on the Governing Council's official register with the seal-points. However, this variety has now been given separate registrations, and comes under the heading of Breed No. 24B.

The chocolate-pointed Siamese is certainly fascinating. It is rather smaller than the other types, with a beautiful pale cream coat and points the colour of milk chocolate. Some very attractive specimens have been making their appearance lately, and at the Southern Counties Championship Show in January 1950 the public were especially fortunate in seeing an entire chocolate-pointed litter, the first to be bred in Britain, or probably the world. These charming kittens were exhibited by the well-known breeder, Mrs. K. R. Williams, of Surrey, who tells me that they have very loving dispositions. And, judging by their behaviour when I was privileged to see them again recently, this certainly appears to be the case.

To conclude this chapter here is the value and standard of points as drawn up by the Siamese Cat Club:

THE SEAL-POINTED CAT

Value of Points
TYPE AND SHAPE • 50
HEAD 15
EARS 5
EYES 5
BODY 15
LEGS AND PAWS 5
TAIL 5

Medium in size, body long and svelte, legs proportionately slim, hind legs slightly higher than front ones, feet small and oval, tail long and tapering (either straight or slightly kinked at the extremity).

Head long and well proportioned, with width between the eyes, narrowing in perfectly straight lines to a fine muzzle, giving the impression of a marten face. Ears, rather large and pricked, wide at the base.

8

COLOUR . . . 50	
EYES 15	Clear, bright and decidedly blue. Shape oriental and slanting towards the nose. No tendency to squint.
BODY COLOUR 10	Cream, shading gradually into pale warm fawn on the back. Kittens paler in colour.
POINTS 10	Mask, ears, legs, feet and tail dense and clearly defined seal brown. Mask complete, and (except in kittens) connected by tracings with the ears.
TEXTURE OF COAT 10	Very short and fine in texture,
CONDITION 5	glossy and close lying.

TOTAL 100

THE BLUE-POINTED CAT

Same as above, with following exceptions:
BODY COLOUR: Glacial white, shading gradually into blue on back, the same cold tone as the points, but of a lighter shade.
EYE COLOUR: Clear, bright china blue.

THE CHOCOLATE-POINTED CAT

TYPE	Same as for seal-pointed cat.
COLOUR POINTS: .	Milk-chocolate colour, the ears, mask, legs, paws and tail to be as even in colour as possible, the ears should not be darker than the points.
EYES	A good china blue (pale slaty eyes to be discouraged).
BODY COLOUR . . .	Ivory colour all over. Shading, if at all, to be the colour of the points. Grey or dingy shading will be a fault.
TEXTURE	As for seal-pointed cat.
CONDITION . . .	As for seal-points.

9

2

Devotion and Loyalty

WHAT *is* the attraction of Siamese cats? Their noisy, rasping voices, thieving ways, mischievousness, and obstinate determination—all these might make them, surely, the least popular among our feline friends. Instead, within three years, from the end of 1946, more than 8,000 of these royal aristocrats were registered with the Governing Council of the Cat Fancy.

But perhaps the reason is not so very hard to find. In character, the Siamese cat is individual as its lovely, svelte appearance. Anyone who has ever reared a Siamese kitten will tell you that its loyalty and devotion surpass those of any other domestic animal, even including dogs.

These charming pets adore their owners with an almost jealous passion. Indeed, many of them fret and go off their food if separated for a day. They will follow you about the house, accompany you on a walk, and are always glad to start a conversation. My own Siamese is very vocal. He has about twenty different "miaous", each with a different shade of meaning.

Contrary to general belief, all Siamese cats are not greedy; neither are they all thieving. One well-known fancier has told of how she was called out urgently, and, so that her cat could have his lunch, she arranged for someone to open the kitchen door for him around noon, having previously put his meal ready on the floor. But on her return she was greeted with the news that the little cat seemed unhappy and had not touched his food. In her haste, his mistress had forgotten to put it in his special dish, and it was still on the plate in which she had prepared it!

My own cat would never take food not offered to him. I have proved this many times. For example, my telephone happens to be fixed in a study upstairs, and on several occasions someone has called me up while I was either putting meat in the oven or serving out a fish meal or some other delicacy that Cæsar loves. Forgetting he was about, I have left the food to answer the telephone, but never once has he attempted to touch it.

This is not to say that Siamese cats are faultless. They can be terribly destructive, and, unless trained to do otherwise, will derive the keenest pleasure from such antics as ripping up the curtains or sharpening their claws on your most expensive furniture. Even their amusing vocal efforts can be a trial to strangers, for there is nothing more infuriating than the high-pitched crescendo of a discontented Siamese.

But allowing for a few minor disturbances during the early days of ownership, no animal could be more worth cultivating. In spite of the strictest rules regarding "show points", no two Siamese cats are ever quite alike. Even tiny kittens soon develop individual personalities. For example, there is the adaptable Siamese who is so affectionate that it will purr loudly and talk to anyone, gaily jumping on the lap of the most ardent felinophobe. On the other hand, there is the highly nervous cat who will spit and swear at any stranger who comes within its reach; there is also the routine cat who dislikes any kind of change in its well-ordered life, the thoughtful, concentrating cat who sits gazing into the fire for hours on end, and so on.

Much has been written about the Siamese cat's intelligence: how it will fetch and carry balls, sit up and beg, shake hands at the command, and so on. But perhaps the most amazing story is of the little seven months' old kitten, who, after accompanying her master on a visit to a friend, literally led him home over a mile and a half of open countryside during a thick fog which had rapidly descended while they were out.

On first acquaintance with a Siamese cat, you may imagine that it has a ferocious disposition. Indeed, with its unusual, lean appearance and Oriental, slanting eyes, the Siamese, more than any other breed of cat, is inclined to resemble its giant relation, the lion. It certainly runs rather like a lion cub, and when perturbed can also roar like one.

Here, however, the resemblance ends, for not only is the Siamese cat companionable and intelligent, but it is gentle too. As a rule, the great wealth of this animal's affection is reserved for just one member of the household, generally the cat's owner. For this privileged person will your Siamese sit hour upon hour and wait, and when finally he appears, the cat will run to greet him purring approval and using its tail to show pleasure as eloquently as any dog would. But do not imagine that Siamese cats will accept injustice easily. They are the most sensitive of creatures. Mr. Beverley Nichols has described how you can depress his cat "One" merely by frowning at him, while you can put his other cat "Four" into a black mood by the mere tone of your voice. My own cat, Cæsar, does not easily forgive even the most gentle of rebukes.

In spite of their tremendous vocal powers, nightly concerts on the tiles do not appear to attract Siamese cats overmuch. Indeed, many of these royal felines seem happier when sleeping peacefully on their owners' beds. My own cat always sleeps downstairs, but never fails to call us regularly at 6.30 every morning, when he appears outside the bedroom door and "miaous" gently to be let in. If he gets no response at once, then he really starts in earnest, gradually working up to a high-pitched crescendo, threatening to rouse the neighbourhood if he is not admitted and allowed on to the bed without further delay.

Many Siamese love travelling about with their owners. One little cat I know accompanies her mistress everywhere. Buses, trains, cars, tubes—nothing seems to daunt her. Not a bit frightened of noise or other passengers, she will sit quietly on my friend's lap without having to be put on a lead or restrained in any way. Car rides appear to be the greatest treat, especially if she can sit up and look out of the window.

But besides a love of human companionship, Siamese also show great affection for each other. The sight of kittens playing is a source of never-ending interest and amusement. Watch them charge about the room, chase each other's tails and knock against all kinds of obstacles until eventually they tire themselves out. Even then they are usually to be found curled up in the same chair or basket.

To say that Siamese cats are artful is putting it mildly. In his delightful book, *Charles: The Story of a Friendship*, Michael Joseph tells how he played a trick on his famous pet: "He had been given something uninteresting—I think it was cold fish—but rightly suspected that the remains of yesterday's pheasant were in the larder. When he put on his usual act, silently grumbling and touching the fish as though it would poison him if he ate it, I pretended not to notice and quickly went out of the room. Tiptoeing back, I peered through the crack in the half-closed door to see Charles wolfing the fish as though he had never tasted or wanted anything better."

In a different way, my own cat has shown me this artful trait of character. Like most Siamese, he has a finicky appetite, and I do try to vary his food as much as possible. One day, however, when meat was unobtainable, I was obliged to give Cæsar fish for two meals in succession. At lunch-time all went well. He ate the fish and apparently enjoyed it. But by supper-time he was already tired of it and "miaoued" loudly for something different to be put down in its place. Finding I would not give in, he sniffed disdainfully and went out into the garden, presently to return with a little tabby kitten, who made straight for Cæsar's dish and hastily cleared up all the food. As a rule, he will not allow another cat near the house, let alone to enter and eat his supper. Once the stranger had departed well-satisfied, Cæsar "miaoued" up at me as if to say, "Now, what about that meat?"

3

Buying a Kitten

THE best time of year to buy a Siamese kitten is the spring. Although Siamese cats are not delicate now, as they were when first imported, the fact remains that our British winter climate, with its fogs and biting winds, is hardly advantageous to the growth of any young thing. The summer gives your kitten a real chance to grow up strong and healthy in the warm sunshine and fresh air. I well remember how, when Cæsar was a tiny kitten, he would spend nearly all day in the garden hiding among bushes and rushing about in the long grass. But even if you are a flat-dweller, your little cat will still benefit from the warm weather. How it will love to play in sunlit corners or stretch out luxuriously and sleep.

Where should you obtain your Siamese kitten? Undoubtedly, the easiest way is from a pet-shop. You see the dearest little kitten in the window. It looks at you rather wistfully, as if to say: "I do so want a garden and trees to climb. Won't you have me?"

Well, provided it is a healthy kitten, there is no reason why you shouldn't give the little fellow a good home. Much has been written against pet-shops, but some of them are excellent enough. I know the proprietors of several such establishments. They are genuinely fond of animals, keep their premises clean, and certainly appear to look after their livestock while it is with them. Yet it is well to realise the risks of buying from any but a recommended dealer.

Kittens may have anything wrong with them, from digestive ailments, through being weaned wrongly or too early, to the far more serious stomach troubles, like cocci-diosis. They may be flea-ridden; others have a persistent form of diarrhœa. And this is not necessarily a stigma on the owner of the pet-shop, for even quite serious ailments are not always apparent on first examination. Who has not heard of the kitten which seemed perfectly well when it was bought, but soon after reaching its destination collapsed and died?

No one can deny that there are many unscrupulous pet-dealers whose premises are breeding quarters for germs. Fake pedigrees have been known, or female kittens sold as males, to mention but two vices designed to exploit the unwary.

Where, then, should you buy your Siamese kitten? I myself would deal only with a breeder direct. If you do not know of any reputable breeder, why not get in touch with the Hon. Secretary of the Siamese Cat Club, Mrs. E. Hart? Her address is: Tye Cottage, Frog Grove Lane, Wood Street, Guildford, Surrey. Mrs. Hart may be able to give you the names and addresses of breeders in or nearest to your own district. Both for your own and the kitten's sake, it is advisable to select a breeder as near your home as possible. Not only are long train journeys frightening for a tiny kitten, but the high-pitched crescendo it may well keep up on the way may be somewhat embarrassing to yourself.

Alternatively, there are several specialist periodicals that cater exclusively for cat-lovers, details of which will be found at the end of this book. Many of the breeders advertise in one or more of these magazines whenever they have stock for sale. Some of them run a permanent advertisement all the year round.

In my own case, I bought my first Siamese kitten at a cat show. It is always a good idea to visit at least one championship show before making up your mind. The reason for doing this is that, even if you do not actually decide upon any particular kitten that day, you should see a number of the best type of specimens and you will at least gain some knowledge as to what is really worth purchasing when the time arrives. Also, shows give one the opportunity of getting to know other fanciers personally. From them you can pick up many useful hints as to the best way of rearing your future Siamese. Do not be afraid to ask questions, for cat-breeders are the most friendly people.

Although there is a special show for kittens and neuter cats held during the summer months, practically all the others take place between October and February each year.[1] This is because the cats are in the best possible condition for exhibition purposes during the winter. Siamese cats

[1] Since this was written, the first Crystal Cat Show was held at Olympia, London, in September, 1950, and is expected to become an annual event.

17

develop lovely, sleek coats in the cold weather, but some do not always look so good in the summer-time because of the spring moult. Broadly speaking, this applies to other breeds of cats too.

At all the shows, with the exception of the annual Championship Show for Blue Persian cats, there is bound to be a very good selection of Siamese. But if you can manage to attend the Siamese Cat Club's own Championship Show, which is usually held during October every year, then you will have a splendid opportunity for studying this fascinating breed all on its own.

Whether you fall in love with a kitten at a show or prefer to contact a breeder privately, never be afraid of asking questions. A breeder will not object to your examining any kitten thoroughly. The fact that you do so proves that you are particular, and therefore likely to give the kitten a good home. State frankly whether you want a male or female, and for what purpose you require the kitten. For example: Are you thinking of breeding from it? Does exhibiting interest you? Or is your Siamese wanted simply as a pleasant companion?

As a rule, a female kitten is slightly cheaper than a male, unless, of course, it promises special qualities, when it may be very much more expensive. At the time of writing, you should be able to buy a seal- or blue-pointed kitten of the companion variety from about 4 to 8 guineas. For a prize-winning kitten or one for breeding purposes, you may have to pay considerably more.

But there are several other reasons for making your intentions clear to the breeder, apart from the question of price. Suppose, for example, that a kitten has a very dark coat, fails in eye colour, has a decided squint, light points, and a kinky tail. Obviously such a specimen will not go very far at a show cat, but there is no reason why it should not make a very lovable pet. Moreover, a breeder is often willing to sell a kitten with one or more such faults very reasonably indeed, so long as it is assured of a good home.

Do not worry if the kitten you fall in love with happens to be a female. Nowadays she can be made neuter with the very minimum of risk. Siamese females are extremely sweet and affectionate; indeed, many people prefer what is known as the spayed female to the neutered male. Incidentally, if you can afford to start off with two kittens, this is always a good plan. Siamese cats have a tremendous affection for each other and will settle down much more easily in new surroundings with companionship. Then think what delight you can have watching the two of them play!

But suppose that you definitely want a show specimen or to go in for breeding. Well, the standard of points to look for has been described in a previous chapter. But do remember that a kitten rarely shows all its qualities when it is very young. Many an adult cat has caused fanciers to shake their heads sadly, lamenting that they had sold it in kittenhood. The now famous Siamese Champion Inwood Shadow did not impress judges very much when she was very young. For one reason, her front paws were rather late in darkening. Once her owner got her into show condition, however, she went from strength to strength until at the National Cat Club Championship Show of 1949, she was easily acclaimed as the best in the show.

For whatever reason you may wish to own a Siamese, you will certainly want a healthy one. At eight to ten weeks old —and it is not advisable to buy a kitten younger—your little cat should weigh about 2 lb. Make sure it is alert and lively, sturdy on its feet, with a soft, glossy-looking coat and bright, healthy eyes. If it happens to be one of a litter, watch it push its brothers and sisters aside for the best share of a feed. This is the kitten that will get into endless mischief once you get it home. How it will try to claw the furniture! But it is not likely to run you into heavy veterinary expense.

Even so, there are still a few further items that might well be investigated before you finally make the purchase. For example, it is always advisable to look at a kitten's ears. Whether it be just dirt or the more serious matter of canker, the merest glance will show. The same applies to fleas. You have only to part the fur to know if a cat is flea-ridden. Again, some kittens appear to suffer from a persistent form of diarrhœa, and although this is usually curable, it needs considerable patience. Far better make sure there is no such trouble in the first place.

Having asked all your own questions, it is now the breeder's turn. Do not be offended if he or she wants to know a few details of the kitten's future environment. After all, he has had all the trouble of rearing your new pet through the early and most difficult weeks of its young life. Most fanciers look upon cat-breeding as something far more than mere commercialism. In fact, I know several fanciers who would never part with any kittens if they could help it, but, of course, there comes a time when numbers just have to be reduced.

IX.   Sukianga Champagne and Sukianga Celeste, at the age of four months. Sukianga Celeste (lying down) is now in Malaya where she was exported by her breeder Mrs. J. Varcoe of Kent, in October, 1949.

X   Seal-pointed Siamese Kittens.

Let us assume, then, that everything is settled quite satisfactorily for both parties. Before departing with your kitten, do make sure to ask for all particulars regarding the diet it has been getting. This is not to say that gradual changes cannot be made with a kitten's food, but it is essential that the breeder's instructions on this matter should be carried out at least during the first few days in new surroundings, or stomach upsets may result.

Before completing the purchase, you will be given a copy of the kitten's pedigree, and at last you are ready to take your kitten home. Wrap it gently in a piece of blanket, and place it in a draughtproof box, which you should take with you for its conveyance. The box should not be so large that when moved the kitten rolls about inside it, but neither should it cramp the kitten's movements. If a basket is used, it is a good idea to cover all four sides with thick brown paper, which should be tied firmly in place with string. Such a precaution not only helps to shut out frightening sights and sounds, but also does a good deal towards eliminating draughts. Naturally, if a box is used, you will see that the top is so arranged as to give the kitten plenty of air.

If your little Siamese is rather noisy on the journey home, do not let it worry you. After all, you are still a stranger, and the shriek of railway trains or noise of street traffic and so on must be very alarming to a baby cat which has only just left its mother. Even so, harden your heart against taking it out of the box for an occasional petting. And I would also resist the temptation of showing off the little darling to every fellow traveller who may ask you for "just one peep". It is very easy for a tiny kitten to catch cold.

4

Rearing the Kitten

BEFORE you bring your Siamese kitten home, you must decide where it is going to sleep. Most people provide a sleeping box or basket and arrange this so that it is slightly off the ground and therefore free from draughts. Of course, your kitten may look upon such plans with utter scorn, forsaking the nice warm blanket you have placed so carefully inside the basket for less comfortable sleeping quarters, such as the top of a sideboard or a mantelshelf! My cat has never yet used the spacious wooden box that I obtained, with considerable difficulty, from the grocer, preferring to choose his own quarters. Even the offer of a cushion in his favourite spot of the moment does not appeal; he just yawns and moves over to another corner. Siamese cats are like that.

This is not to say that these cats can't be trained to go to a special bed. Naturally, you may not want your kitten to lie around in *any* place that takes its fancy. But the chief point to remember is that the kitten should be kept warm.

For this reason, a box is really a better proposition than a basket, for it is less likely to let in draughts. However, if you do prefer a basket, then it is a good idea to line the bottom and the sides of it.

Regarding the bedding, this is really a matter of personal preference. Some people go to any amount of trouble for pedigree cats, even to the extent of providing them with coloured blankets, fancy cushions and so on. Such extravagance is quite unnecessary. In fact, by rights, no cat should be allowed to sleep on cushions unless these are equipped with loose covers that can be washed very frequently. Otherwise, they are likely to become a breeding place for fleas.

It is far better to use layers of ordinary newspaper, and place a piece of old but clean blanket or towelling over them. Newspaper on its own will provide all the necessary warmth, but the covering is advisable just in case the cat gets any of the print on its coat. Should this happen, and it is licked off, a stomach upset may be the consequence.

So much for the kitten's bed. How are you going to feed it? Let us assume your little pet has just left its mother and is from about eight to twelve weeks old. At such a tender age a kitten cannot digest very much food at a time. So your policy is little and often. During these early days breeders advise four very small meals a day.

In regard to diet itself, this is such a controversial question that I do not consider any hard-and-fast rules can be laid down. For example, many Siamese kittens do not like milk, but that hardly seems a reason to begrudge them all this delicacy. Again, some people will tell you that green vegetables are an essential part of the diet, yet a number of

Siamese cats who will not touch them do thrive. There is only one solution: Find out exactly what your kitten has been eating and keep to this diet strictly until it has settled down. Then, if you like, you can make a few changes gradually.

Of course, the most important item in any cat's diet should be flesh food, and the Siamese is certainly no exception to this rule. Tiny kittens can be given a little minced meat (either raw or cooked) with complete safety. They may have baked or boiled fish with all the bones taken out, cooked rabbit with the bones removed, and so on. Your kitten will also enjoy a little minced liver or whale-meat occasionally, and Siamese just relish a non-splinter bone. The sight of Cæsar running up the garden with a bone in his mouth is the source of amusement among many of our friends. "A real doggy cat!" they call him. Or: "Whoever heard of a cat with a bone!"

As it happens, all kittens should be given a bone to gnaw, especially when they are teething. Not only will the persistent action of biting on to something hard help the new teeth through the gums, but it will keep your kitten away from the precious furniture and curtains. Of course, you must never, on any account, give a kitten poultry bones. These can be very dangerous if they splinter and lodge in the throat. A veterinary surgeon once told me that more cats were brought to him for this reason than any other.

It may help if I give a rough idea of Cæsar's diet when I first had him as a kitten. He was on a strict four-meals-a-day routine, two of which were milky foods and the others of a flesh basis. For example, supposing breakfast consisted of a little fish mixed with a few cornflakes, then he might have brown bread and milk or a cereal mixed with milk for lunch. For the evening meal (the biggest of the day) I would give him either a little minced beef, fish with all the bones removed, rabbit, horseflesh, or whale-meat—in fact, anything I could get in that line. Then at bedtime he would have another milky meal. To the main meal of the day I would add two drops of halibut-liver oil. This, of course, contains vitamin D, which helps to develop strong bones and prevents such complications as rickets. It should be realised that the above is only intended as a rough guide. Many Siamese owners prefer to reverse my method and feed a milky meal for breakfast and something in the flesh variety during the day. It all depends on how your kitten has been weaned and the diet it thrives on best.

One very important point, however, is emphasised by all breeders: the necessity for regular meal-times. Find out the times at which your kitten has been fed, and if possible keep to them. If such times are really inconvenient, then fix others to suit yourself, but make the alteration permanent. As with humans, nothing is worse for a cat's digestion than varied meal-times and scraps between meals.

Do remember that if you can get some liver occasionally, this is excellent for your kitten's health. Boiled or lightly grilled, liver helps the organs to function and wards off constipation. At the risk of sounding over-optimistic in these days of scarcity, I must add the warning that too much of this diet causes diarrhœa. So even when better times return and you can get plenty of liver, keep it as a special treat for your kitten, once or twice a week.

So far no real mention has been made of green vegetables, which are useful additions to a kitten's diet. Unfortunately, many Siamese, in common with some other cats, will not eat them. Cæsar was always a grave offender in this respect, and nothing has ever induced him to change his mind. Yes, I have tried mincing the vegetables with his meat, but he sniffs disdainfully and leaves the lot! But, frankly, if your own kitten proves troublesome in this respect, I would not let it worry you. At least one of our foremost breeders never gives her cats vegetables, believing that carnivorous animals fare best when they are fed as near as possible to Nature.

After all, we need only think of the wild cat, which, in its natural state, catches birds for sustenance and drinks from streams. It is very doubtful whether it has ever tasted boiled vegetables or milk. And while on the subject of milk, I would like to point out that too much of this can prove harmful to any cat. It has been known to set up serious gastric troubles and even skin disease.

Very few Siamese cats like cow's milk, although I find they usually enjoy the tinned, unsweetened, evaporated milk or almost any of the proprietary milk foods. If you can get goat's milk, so much the better. Practically all kittens thrive on this. But the best and cheapest drink for any cat is water, so always have a small bowl handy. Change it twice a day or even more during the hot weather. Apart from quenching thirst, water acts as a natural aperient. Even when ill and off their food, most cats will lap water.

As your kitten grows, it will be able to take larger meals, so you can gradually decrease the number. Broadly speaking, from five to nine months old three meals a day should be sufficient, and from then onwards two meals a day. A few adult cats do thrive better on three small meals rather than two large ones, but these are the exceptions. Of course, invalids are fed differently and a slight distinction may be necessary for nursing mothers, but these will be discussed in later chapters.

It is quite impossible to say exactly how much food an adult cat requires at each meal. As with humans, appetites vary considerably. As a rough guide, take 4-6 oz. of meat or fish per day and mix this with brown bread crumbs, biscuit meal, or green vegetables. Try to vary the diet as much as possible. Who wouldn't get tired of the same old thing put down day after day?

Whether you feed meat raw or cooked is another controversial matter. Personally, I feel it depends on how the cat likes it. Most Siamese are fond of raw meat, and as long as it is perfectly fresh there is no need to cook any of the goodness out of it. Perhaps I have spoilt Cæsar. Friends certainly tell me I have. Anyway, it seems that he would rather starve than eat meat that has not been cooked for him. Of course, no cat should ever be given raw fish.

Most cats know when they have had enough, and it is not advisable to leave food down for long periods. In the hot weather this is especially dangerous, for it encourages flies. There are occasions when a cat may not be particularly hungry at a meal-time. Lack of exercise is often the cause. After sleeping all the morning, my own cat has refused food on many days, but a run in the garden has soon brought back his appetite.

How many cat owners realise that too much white fish is often harmful to their pets? It has been found that any number of feline sufferers from eczema and other skin troubles were those existing almost entirely on a fish diet. On the other hand, sardines, pilchards, silds, brislings, and so on are all very good indeed, the oil being especially beneficial. In addition, I have always given my cats a small spoonful of olive oil occasionally. Not only does this help the organs to function, but prevents hair-ball from collecting and keeps out chills. Most Siamese will lap it up readily.

But to sum up: Remember that where feeding is concerned, meat is the very best basic diet for a Siamese cat. You will not need to sacrifice your ration. Most cats love horse-flesh, and as long as it is absolutely fresh it can be fed to them with complete safety, either cooked or raw. To be quite certain, only buy that sold for human consumption. Always give the food as dry as possible, and never offer a milky meal for at least three hours after meat or stomach troubles will probably result.

Siamese cats are the cleanest of animals, and when you buy a kitten it is almost certain to be house-trained. Nevertheless, it should be provided with a small sanitary tray—something in the nature of a shallow meat-tin—just in case of an emergency. The tray should be filled with dry earth, sifted ashes or peat-moss litter. Some people favour sawdust, but this is inclined to stick to the kitten's fur, and should any be swallowed when your pet licks itself, a stomach upset may follow. When obtainable, I feel that dry earth should always be used, because undoubtedly the cat prefers it. But during the bad weather peat-moss litter makes a good substitute and is very easily disposed of. For flat-dwellers, peat-moss litter is probably the best all the year round.

Always keep the sanitary tray in exactly the same place: fairly near the sleeping box is as good a spot as any. A kitten that knows just where to find its tray will run there immediately it is required. To change the place continually is asking for trouble. It bewilders the kitten and encourages it to be dirty.

Naturally, you will keep the tray scrupulously clean, disinfecting it from time to time and changing the material in it daily. Cats are extremely fastidious and would rather suffer discomfort than use a dirty tray. Should a young kitten misbehave, by all means rebuke it gently. However, do not imagine that you can train it by slapping it or that other senseless habit of rubbing its nose in the mess. Neither action will cure the trouble and you will only make your kitten nervous.

Like any other cat, the Siamese is very particular about its toilet. Once Cæsar starts to wash himself, we often wonder whenever he is going to stop. Over and over again his rough little tongue goes up and down each dark brown paw, then slowly but determinedly he begins on the rest of his anatomy, until, after repeated polishings of this part and that, eventually he is finished.

All the same, if your pet is to look really well-groomed, a little help on your part will be necessary. This especially applies during the moulting season, when regular brushing and combing will help to remove the loose hairs and so minimise the risk of them collecting in the cat's stomach when it licks itself.

Unlike some cats, Siamese love being brushed and combed. In fact, they love any attention you can give them. I find a wooden bench a good place for my cat's toilet, but the kitchen table with newspaper spread over it would do equally well. Use a steel comb with fine, short teeth, and with this gently remove all the loose hairs. Then brush fairly vigorously from head to tail, using a stiff-bristled brush for the purpose. Finish off with a silk pad or piece of chamois leather, which will give your pet a beautiful, glossy appearance.

Don't forget the underpart of the cat's body, and always pay special attention to the fur round the ears, under the chin, and all four legs. It is in these parts that dust and insects are most likely to collect. About once a week I usually comb my cat with a little water to which a few drops of Milton or Dettol have been added. This is especially recommended during the summer months, when, even with the most careful grooming, a cat is liable to pick up an odd flea. If preferred, you can use one of the various insect powders on the market. But whatever you decide on, make absolutely certain that the container is labelled as harmless to domestic pets, and never on any account use D.D.T. on cats. This is harmless enough in its dry state, but may prove fatal if the cat licks itself.

At weekly intervals I also clean my cat's ears. This is something your pet cannot possibly manage for itself and, if neglected, may be an immediate cause of canker, which is most painful for the cat and often extremely difficult to cure. To clean a cat's ears is perfectly simple, and if it is accustomed to the treatment from an early age, co-operation will be given willingly. All traces of dirt can be removed quite easily with a little Antepeol ointment or diluted hydrogen peroxide on

XI. Doneraile Dandy (right) and Doneraile Delia, bred by Mrs. K. R. Williams of Sutton, Surrey. Both these kittens were exported to U.S.A., where Dandy attained his Championship at eleven months old. The picture shows the kittens at the Kensington Kitten and Neuter Cat Club's Show, at Bayswater, London, when they were three months old.

XII. Prize-winning kittens bred by Mrs. Joan B. Varcoe of Kent. Picture was taken at the National Cat Club's Championship Show in December, 1949. The kittens won first prize.

cotton-wool wrapped round the tip of an orange stick. Insert this very gently into the cat's ear, paying careful attention to the crevices. Be sure to do this very tenderly because the ear is a most delicate organ. The eyes should also be wiped gently with cotton-wool every day.

Most cats hate water and, apart from very exceptional circumstances, should not be bathed. However, if it really is necessary to wash your pet (a chimney adventure may give just cause), then be very careful how you do it and make sure the cat is properly dried. You will need a fairly deep bowl to stand the cat in and a good lather of pure soft soap. Carbolic or coal-tar soaps are not advised. Make sure the water is not too hot; then rub the lather well into your pet's coat, leaving the washing of its head until the last. Get someone to hold the cat while you change the water. Do this as quickly as possible or the animal may catch cold. After rinsing in clean, warm water, wrap the cat in a warm, dry towel and dry thoroughly. Do not on any account let it out after bathing, and try to persuade it to remain near the fire for an hour or so at least. A drink of warm milk also helps to minimise any risk of chill.

All cats should have access to grass, which is their natural medicine. Not only does it relieve stomach disorders, but it acts as an emetic and is often the means of inducing the cat to vomit hair-ball, which, if retained in the stomach, can be very dangerous. Cats which enjoy entire freedom usually manage to obtain all the grass they want, but flat-dwellers should grow some for their pets' needs. The best variety is cocksfoot, and this can be grown satisfactorily in pots of any size, but a pot about 6 or 8 ins. across the top is most convenient for handling. You may prefer to use shallow boxes, about 12 ins. long, 10 ins. wide, and 3 ins. deep. These also should serve the purpose very well. Sufficient seed to sow six pots of grass, with full instructions for growing it, can be obtained from the Cats' Protection League, 29 Church Street, Slough, Bucks. There is no charge made for this service apart from the usual stamp to cover postage.

Opinions differ as to why kittens sharpen their claws. Some authorities consider they do it to stretch the muscles of their legs. Whatever the reason, Siamese are the worst offenders, so, unless you want the furniture ruined, provide your pet with a useful scratching implement. The best idea I know of is a stout piece of wood about 18 ins. by 12 ins., covered with hessian or old carpeting which has been nailed firmly round the edges. Friends with several Siamese cats tell me that their pets can all be trained quite easily to use this type of board, whereas other kinds made absolutely no impression.

But there is no denying that the claws of a Siamese occasionally become uncontrollable. Then, during play, they are apt to scratch even those they are most fond of. If this happens, the only thing to do is to trim the claws. But use special nail-clippers, and only take the merest point off or you may split the nail.

Siamese cats like to be picked up and petted, but if you have children in the house do see that they handle the kitten gently. Only recently a young mother boasted that the cat was never allowed any rest until her little son had gone to bed. She added laughingly: "It's not that he does not love the kitten. He just thinks of it as a toy!" Children who grow up in homes where animals are really loved learn to regard them as companions, not as playthings.

Unfortunately, many adults never bother to pick a cat up properly. It should be lifted gently by placing one hand behind its front legs and the other under its hind quarters. If done in that way, the cat is practically in a sitting position and does not suffer any discomfort when held. Never lift a cat so that its head and feet are dangling. These suggestions, of course, apply to any breed of cat, not only to the Siamese.

You cannot always be playing with your kitten, so be sure to provide it with a few toys. Kittens will romp merrily with a ping-pong ball, an empty cotton reel, or even a piece of stiff paper. Nevertheless, I can't help feeling that the favourite plaything is a cat-nip mouse. You can make one quite easily with grey felt, and your pet will love it. For a specially realistic-looking mouse, I recommend those made by Miss D. J. Ruxton, a member of the Cats' Protection League, and sold in aid of this society's funds. When I first gave one to Cæsar he carried it around with him for days, and even slept with it beside him. To this day he likes nothing better than for someone to throw his mouse up in the air so that he can retrieve it. Enquiries for these mice should be made direct to Miss Ruxton at Martin Lodge, Mayfield, Tunbridge Wells.

Before leaving the subject of toys, never give your kitten wool, woolly balls, painted or rubber objects to play with. Pieces are likely to flake or break off, and if swallowed may set up serious internal trouble.

This chapter is concerned mainly with the pet or domestic

Siamese cat, so it seems a good place to discuss neutering. Some people who live in the country do find that they can keep an un-doctored male Siamese successfully. But for the town-dweller there is always the fear of the cat spraying on curtains, furniture, and so on, owing to its more confined environment. But quite apart from this unpleasant habit, what is there to prevent your pet from roaming off for days at a time in search of females? Who knows what fights he may become involved in on the way, or what germs he may pick up? Far, far better give him the chance of a happy, peaceful life in the sunshine of your own garden or by your fireside.

But get a qualified veterinary surgeon to perform the operation. In competent hands there is little or no risk. Opinions differ as to the best age for castration; my own vet considers that a kitten should be neutered as soon as it is sufficiently mature. Cæsar was neutered when he was just three months old. It is advisable not to leave the operation later than six months old, because from that age the law rightly insists that a general anæsthetic be given and Siamese cats do not always react favourably to this. Some kittens are a little off colour for a few hours after the operation; others begin to play as if nothing had happened. There is no doubt about it that neutered Siamese grow into fine cats and show a very great affection for their owners.

Spaying the female is definitely a more serious matter, for the operation is a much bigger one, entailing the removal of the ovaries. At the same time, one soon realises that it is almost impossible to keep an un-spayed female without mating her. As a rule, she becomes terribly noisy when in heat, and even if *you* could stand it, the neighbours would probably complain. Of course, if you are prepared to let her out at such times your difficulties are over. Nevertheless, this may be cruel. Apart from the fact that she is almost bound to produce a mongrel litter, she is likely to suffer the attentions of every tom-cat in the neighbourhood.

I must admit that if I kept a Siamese female and did not wish to breed from her, I would certainly have her spayed. Eminent veterinary surgeons advise the operation nowadays, and many ardent cat-lovers prefer to keep a spayed female than a neutered male. Undoubtedly spayed Siamese make delightful pets; they are so affectionate and full of character.

The operation can be performed at any age, usually the earlier the better. However, get your veterinary surgeon's advice. It is also advisable to make certain that whoever you place your faith in is not only well qualified, but accustomed to treating and handling cats. Once you have found the right vet, be sure to obey his instructions after the operation. Keep your pet warm for a few days and see that she does not get over-excited. With ordinary common-sense care, she should soon be quite all right.

5

Breeding Siamese Cats

WHAT could be more fun than breeding Siamese kittens? Provided you have the time and necessary accommodation, I can imagine no more delightful hobby. This does not mean that you will need a mansion with acres of land. Siamese cats are bred successfully in small houses and even in flats. But growing kittens do need a room to themselves so that they can run about and play without the risk of being trod upon. Needless to say, this room should be light and airy. In due course, you may like to build a cattery, but this is not really necessary in the early stages.

The time factor is important, because it is far more difficult to raise newly-born kittens than to continue rearing a pet kitten which has already been successfully weaned. During the weaning period, regularity of feeding is essential. Even if *you* can't always be on the spot to give the kittens their meals, someone else must be appointed to do so.

Time also must be found to visit shows, for these are the breeder's shop window. Besides exhibiting your own stock whenever possible, you will need to study that of other fanciers, especially stud cats, with a view to mating your queens. In the Fancy, female cats are known as queens.

The ideal way of beginning is to buy an adult queen which has proven ability as a breeder; and occasionally such a cat is offered for sale. If the queen is a well-known one, she will probably command a very good price, especially if she has done well on the show bench.

However, most novices make a very satisfactory start by purchasing a really good female kitten. One of the advantages of this is that you have the companionship of the animal from infancy—always a delightful time to own any pet. Advice has been given in a previous chapter on buying a kitten, but the aspirant breeder or exhibitor should pay very careful attention to pedigree. If in doubt get the advice of an expert, although if you are buying from one of the established breeders it is usually safe to leave the matter in his or her hands. This is not to suggest that novice breeders can't be trusted, but some of them may have little more real knowledge than yourself. In the early days, we all think our own cats are perfect.

Most queens come into season from about seven or eight months old—"calling" is the term used in the Fancy. Normally, a queen should not be mated until she is about a year old, but occasionally a Siamese will begin calling so early (even at four months old) that it is advisable to find her a husband sooner. However, no queen should ever be mated until she is at least eight months old.

There was a time when I wondered how one knew when a female cat was in season. The very lovable but ordinary tabby I had would go out without giving us any preliminary warning, and in due course would produce a litter of kittens. No one could ever say that the Siamese is like that. Not that she would object to finding her own mate if given a chance, but you could never say she did not warn you. Most Siamese in a love-sick condition are very noisy indeed.

Early symptoms are usually a great show of affection. The cat may roll on the floor, rub herself both against you and the furniture, crouch, and sometimes scrape the ground with her hind feet. As soon as any of these signs are noticed, watch your pet carefully, for you may be almost certain that she will begin calling before long. When this happens, either take or send her to the owner of the stud, with whom you have made arrangements in advance. And do remember it is not enough to find a male Siamese. The stud should be strong in the points where your queen is weak.

To make this clearer, let us suppose your pet has brilliant blue eyes, but, as often happens in such cases, her coat is far too dark. Your job, then, is to find a stud with a very pale, even coat. If your queen has a short tail, the stud should have a long, whip tail and so on.

Pedigree must be studied too. Naturally, just as your cat inherits good and bad qualities from her ancestors, some of these traits will be handed down to her kittens. Going back to the question of eye colour. although your queen has perfect eyes, if some of her ancestors failed in this quality it is more than likely that many of her kittens will do

XIII. Siamese quintette — owned by Mrs. K. Macpherson of Balcombe, Sussex. The scene is the Southern Counties Cat Club Championship Show, Lime Grove Baths, Shepherd's Bush, London, January 30th, 1950.

XIV. Raard Blue Sacchi, Mrs. Macdonald's famous Blue-pointed Stud. 1st Prizewinning B.-P. Stud at the Siamese Cat Club Championship Show, 1948, also Best B.-P. Male Adult in the National Cat Club Class. Winner of the Shenfield Cup Best Stud, any Variety, and many other awards.

Picture Post

XV. Lemling English Rose, bred by Mrs. Ella Martin, of Chelmsford and exported to America to join the famous Siamese cattery of Mr. Price Cross, of Dallas, Texas.

XVI. Lemling
English Rose
obviously has a
sense of adven-
ture and here
she sets out
on her own
account to see
the world.

likewise. Mate her to a stud with the same defect in his pedigree and the possibility is doubled.

Of course, this matter of studying pedigree to real advantage is always rather difficult for the complete novice. Like everything else, it comes with experience. One sees a number of beautiful cats at the shows, and at least a preliminary study can be made on these occasions. But try to be discerning and remember that champions do not necessarily sire the best kittens; so never book a cat merely on the strength of his awards. A list of cats at stud, price 3*d*., and also a stud book, price 3*s*., can be obtained from the Secretary of the Governing Council of the Cat Fancy, Mr. W. A. Hazeldine, 1 Roundwood Way, Banstead, Surrey.

Although one wants to choose the best cat possible, personally I would not select one that necessitates too long a journey unless I was prepared to take the queen myself. I must admit that I would never allow a pet of mine to travel anywhere unaccompanied, but probably this is prejudice, because many cats are sent on long journeys by railway and arrive quite safely. Also stud-owners are very good about meeting queens at the various termini.

But however your queen is going to travel, a suitable draughtproof box or basket will be necessary. This can be similar to that described in Chapter 3, but, naturally, on a much larger scale. If the cat is journeying unaccompanied, then be sure to fasten the carrier securely. You would never forgive yourself if she escaped.

Paste a label right across the hamper: "LIVE CAT, KEEP OUT OF DRAUGHTS", and also mark the basket "TO BE CALLED FOR". The station clerk at the terminus will then notify the stud-owner of the cat's arrival, which will save much unnecessary delay. Another label should bear the name and address (in block letters) of both stud-owner and sender, and telephone numbers should be inserted where possible.

Railway charges for livestock vary, but if you pay the higher rate and also insure the animal, this will make certain of its being looked after on the journey. Always notify the stud-owner, either by telephone or wire, the time of the cat's departure and approximate time of arrival. Stud fees average from £2 to £3 and are payable in advance.

It will take your queen a little while to get used to the new surroundings, so do not expect her back for several days. The stud-owner will let you know when the cat is being returned.

Do not give your pet her full freedom at once, even if she has left off calling. It is always possible that the mating has proved unsuccessful, and if the queen gets out she may well present you with a mongrel litter. Of course, accidents do happen, and should your Siamese have hybrid kittens do not imagine that she can never produce a pure-bred litter again. Rest her for a while and then mate her to a Siamese stud. If satisfactory, the result will be pedigree kittens.

About four weeks should show whether the mating has been successful. The cat's nipples swell slightly and assume a pinkish colour. But in any case, if the journey has proved futile, the queen will almost certainly have called again in the meanwhile. In such circumstances most stud-owners will give a second mating free of charge, but, of course, there is no obligation for them to do so.

The gestation period is from sixty-three to sixty-five days, but in most cases the kittens arrive on the sixty-fifth day. A few queens carry their young for a slightly longer duration, but if there are no signs of labour by the sixty-eighth day it is advisable to consult a vet.

Do not make an invalid of your pet during this gestation time. If necessary, worm her before mating, but not afterwards. Breeders do not advise worming a pregnant queen. There is no need to restrict the cat's liberty in any way, as fresh air and exercise are both important during pregnancy. Animals have a wonderful sense of intuition, and your pet will soon know if she is attempting more than she can manage.

Regarding food, no alteration is necessary for the first few weeks of the pregnancy but after this period an extra meal should be given daily. It is a good idea to give Lactol for this additional meal, for this increases and improves the supply of milk. Strong aperients should be avoided, but occasionally a small dose of medicinal paraffin oil is beneficial.

Anyone who has kept a female cat will know that she always tries to choose her own bed for confinements. I once had a queen which always selected my best hat-box. All the same, you should provide a comfortable bed well ahead of the event, so that you can get your Siamese used to the idea when you find her slinking into the wrong places.

A very good bed can be made from a cardboard or wooden box about 24 ins. wide by 16 ins. deep. Construct it so that it is open or partly open at the front, and raise it slightly off the floor. Line the box with an old piece of blanket covered with sheets of newspaper. Then place it in a corner of the least inhabited room, well away from the light.

It is always wise to hang a small curtain across the front of the box. Not only will this give the queen more privacy, but it will protect the kittens' eyes.

Most Siamese have their babies quite easily, so do not disturb your pet unless she seems to want you near her. Some cats love to have their owners by them at this time, but others like to be left alone. However, it is always advisable to remain on the premises, just in case anything should go wrong. No one can say exactly how long the family will take to arrive, because queens vary considerably in this matter. Once the first kitten is born, the others usually come in fairly quick succession. But should there be no signs of the first kitten in about two hours from the commencement of labour, it might be wise to call a vet. This especially applies if the queen seems exhausted, or continually gets out of her box and tries to expel the kitten while walking round the room.

Each kitten is born in a separate sac, which normally the mother cat rends with her teeth. She bites through the umbilical cord to free the baby. However, very occasionally a maiden queen will be so nervous that she fails to do this, in which case you must come to her rescue immediately if the kitten is to be saved. It is perfectly easy to split the sac open by using the finger and thumb of both hands. Hold the cord firmly between the finger and thumb of the left hand, and with the right hand very gently pull the cord where it is nearest to the placenta.[1] You will find it will break quite easily.

[1] Placenta: the "afterbirth"—a spongy organ nourishing the fœtus in mammals and expelled after the birth.

As a rule, the mother will then start to clean up. She licks the kitten, and the roughness of her tongue puts life into it, so that it usually begins to cry. Should the queen fail even in this part of her duty, then try rubbing the kitten hard with a rough towel. To clear away the mucus, gently insert a finger into the kitten's mouth. Then wrap the kitten in a piece of blanket, and place it in a box with a covered hot-water bottle until the remainder of the family have arrived.

But Siamese cats make good mothers, and rarely is there need for interference. Once your pet has settled with her kittens, give her a drink of milk and creep away. Later on will be time enough to change the bedding, when, without disturbing the family more than is absolutely necessary, you remove the soiled newspapers and put a clean blanket in their place. It is a good idea to sprinkle a little insect powder underneath the bedding. This will keep the kittens free of fleas. But be sure it is placed *underneath*, and never use D.D.T.

Some people find it difficult to sex young kittens. The easiest time to do this is within the first twenty-four hours of their birth. New fanciers are advised to obtain the excellent sex diagram, price 3*d*., issued by the Cats' Protection League, 29 Church Street, Slough, Bucks.

Feed your queen well while she is nursing her babies, but do not give meat for the first twenty-four hours. Instead, let her have as much milky food as she will take. Usually a queen will eat all the placentas, which not only act as a purgative, but encourage the flow of milk. Should there be any difficulty with the milk, try massaging the teats with a little olive oil. If this does not suffice, then send for the vet.

Most Siamese have large litters, and it may not be good

43

for your pet to feed all the kittens herself. Before the war, when pedigree cats were not nearly so popular as they are to-day, breeders were often compelled to have many of the female kittens destroyed at birth. Nowadays, this is rarely necessary. Even kittens unfit for breeding can always be neutered as pets.

So a possible solution is a foster-mother. If you do not know anyone who may be willing to lend you a mother cat, an advertisement in the columns of one of the newspapers often brings good results. Of course, you must be very careful about the cat you admit into your house or cattery. Always inspect carefully for fleas, ear-canker, and skin trouble.

Leave both cats all their own kittens for a day or two, as it is better that the pedigree litter should have their own mother's milk just at first. The introduction should then be made very carefully. Siamese kittens are born quite white, so will probably look entirely different from the foster's babies. If she takes a dislike to the little strangers, she may refuse to have anything to do with them or even turn them out.

Wait until the foster leaves her family for a while, then replace several of her kittens with the same number of Siamese. It is a good idea to rub the pedigree babies lightly against those of the foster so that all the kittens smell alike. When the mother cat returns, watch her reactions carefully. If she settles down to wash the new kittens, you may be sure she has taken to them and you can safely leave her. Usually there is no trouble in this respect.

Of course, you will have the mongrel kittens destroyed as

humanely as possible. Drowning is *not* a good method of disposing of unwanted kittens, for even at this tender age the death is prolonged and painful. Get a vet or animal clinic to have the babies put to sleep. The small fee will be well spent. After all, their mother has done you a good service.

But occasionally a queen may be too ill to nurse any of her kittens. If a foster is unobtainable, the only thing to do is to try rearing them by hand. But be prepared for hard work, as a good deal of patience is required. For at least a week the kittens must be fed at two-hourly intervals both day and night. A special type of spoon with teat attached is available for this purpose. If possible, feed goat's milk. Practically all kittens thrive on this. Cow's milk is not nearly concentrated enough for a kitten's needs. If goat's milk cannot be obtained, then get some Sherley's Lactol, which is now being manufactured again, and is the finest substitute.

Warm the food to a temperature of 100° Fahrenheit and allow half a spoonful of mixed Lactol, gradually increasing the quantity as the kitten grows. Feed only one kitten at a time. Begin by smearing its lips with a little food, then squeeze a drop of milk on to the tip of the rubber teat and place this to the kitten's mouth. When about a fortnight old, it will often lap the food out of a spoon, which saves a lot of trouble.

Don't forget to keep the kittens warm. Siamese cats are susceptible to cold and damp at all times, and newly-born kittens especially so. During the early days of their life a well-covered hot-water bottle in their box is a sensible precaution. And when there is no mother cat you must be

45

prepared to attend to the kittens' toilet, so the bedding must be constantly changed.

However, the above suggestions allude to unusual circumstances. Normally, kittens are best left to their mother's care during the first few weeks of their life. And although friends may pester you to see the babies, it is really better to refuse them. The mother cat may resent interference from strangers.

When the kittens are about a week to ten days old their eyes will begin to open. Examine carefully to make sure there is no inflammation. If the lids appear at all sore or sticky, gently bathe them with warm boracic lotion, and then smear on just a touch of vaseline or golden eye ointment.

The age you begin to wean the kittens rather depends upon the size of the litter. If a large one, most breeders advise weaning when the kittens are about three weeks old. Should there be only two or three kittens (although this is unusual with Siamese), then you can wait a little longer. Always use goat's milk if you can get it. Otherwise, Sherley's Lactol or one of the other patent milk foods for animals. Some breeders do find cow's milk satisfactory, but if this is used a few drops of lime-water should be added.

For the first week give one or two very tiny feeds each day. Take one kitten at a time and proceed as described in the paragraphs on hand-feeding. Of course, with these older kittens your task will be much easier, for you can gently put their noses to the milk and encourage them to lap. But take care not to frighten them. If any of the food gets up their noses and makes them splutter, they may lose confidence and

46

XVII, XVIII.   Velvet Mask Selina with kittens, owned by Mrs. Linda Parker of Leicester.

XIX. Mrs. Hart with Mrs. Hethering-on's Sealsleeve Petite-Laid, winner of he Open Male Championship at the Siamese Cat Club Championship Show, 947. *Sport & General*

XX. Mrs. Duncan Hindley inspecting the famous kitten Lemling English Rose, only female from a litter of eight, sired by Mrs. Hindley's own Prestwick Penglima Pertama, mentioned in the text. *Picture Post*

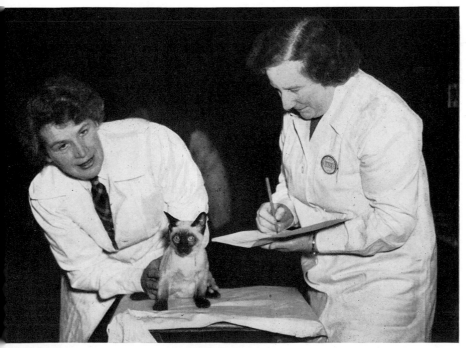

XXI. Hielan Mist submits to the inspection of Mrs. Katrina Sayers (*right*) the well-known judge of Siamese. The cat is held by her steward Mrs. Anne Vize, at the Croydon Cat Club's Championship Show, 1949. *P.A.—Reuter*

will then be discouraged from trying again for some time. Naturally, the kittens will still be feeding from their mother. Increase the food gradually, until, at a month old, the kittens are having four small meals a day. At six weeks old, put them on to a very little solid food, such as fish mashed with milk or finely chopped rabbit with brown bread crumbs. At this age one solid meal a day will be enough. At eight weeks old the kittens can have a very small helping of scraped raw meat, and from that time onwards they should be given two solid meals a day and two milky ones, as described in an earlier chapter.

From the time you start to wean the kittens a sanitary tray will be essential. The mother cat will train them how to use it; all you need to do is put it down. Should a kitten start scratching in an odd corner of the room and its mother is not about, just talk to it gently and put it on the tray. Siamese kittens are trained in no time.

So now your kittens are ready to go to their new homes. But if you want to show any, you may have to keep them all a little longer to see how they develop. All kittens look attractive in the baby stage, but it is rare that one can judge their true physical qualities when quite so young. However, do not keep them too long or you won't be able to part with them at all.

No doubt your queen's first litter will sell quite easily, for friends who like your pet will probably want a kitten. I have had to disappoint many of my own acquaintances when I tell them that Cæsar is a neutered male! Later on you may need to advertise your stock, and this can be done either through the columns of a local or national newspaper or in one of the periodicals listed at the end of this book. If you belong to the Siamese Cat Club, or any of the other cat clubs, it is also advisable to let the secretary know that you have kittens for sale.

It always pays to be scrupulously honest with would-be purchasers. We all think our own pets are the most beautiful of any, and in your early days as a fancier it may be difficult to get a true perspective of your stock. If at all in doubt, an experienced breeder will always advise you.

Naturally, you will want good homes for the kittens, but don't be like a friend of mine who refused to sell because the would-be purchasers only had *small* houses. Siamese cats are not snobs. They don't mind in the least whether their owners live in mansions or in stables. What they do ask for is loving care and human companionship.

If your queen starts calling again soon after her first litter, never mate her again immediately. Both for her own sake and that of her future progeny it is most important that she should be well rested between litters. Broadly speaking, two litters each season are enough for any queen.

After a little experience in breeding and exhibiting, you may wish for a stud cat of your own. Give the matter very careful thought, however, for stud work is far from easy. Many breeders do find it extremely interesting, but they all give the same advice for success: plenty of room is absolutely essential, plenty of patience, and, above all, a genuine love of cats.

How will you find your stud cat? For your own females you will need a really good out-cross, for, except in very rare circumstances, inbreeding is not advised. It is seldom

48

that an experienced stud cat is for sale, and when one is available, naturally the price is high. Therefore, the purchase of a young male cat from about six months old is your wisest choice. At this age a cat is beginning to reveal his best qualities both with regards to disposition and physical characteristics.

The matter of temperament is far more important than you may think. A spiteful cat may well pass on this disagreeable trait to many of his kittens, and a stud's reputation is made chiefly on the virtues of his progeny. However, do not expect to find the perfect cat, for such does not exist. What you want is soundness of type, strength of limb, and absence of outstanding faults. A good pedigree is essential.

We have already discussed the unsuitability of keeping a full male cat in the house, so outside premises will be necessary. You will need good-sized draughtproof quarters, which should face south if possible and have well-made windows to let in plenty of air. At the same time, warmth must be provided during the winter months, for damp and draughts are a Siamese cat's worst enemies. For the following suggestions on the stud house I am indebted to Mrs. K. R. Williams of Sutton, Surrey. Mrs. Williams is one of Britain's foremost judges and breeders of Siamese cats. This is what she says:

"Do not buy a house for your stud because you have one offered or can get it cheaply; although expensive, there are more about now. Your stud has to spend a great part of his life in this house, and it is up to you to see he is housed in comfort. Do not set it up without carefully selecting the position: take the run into consideration, and place your

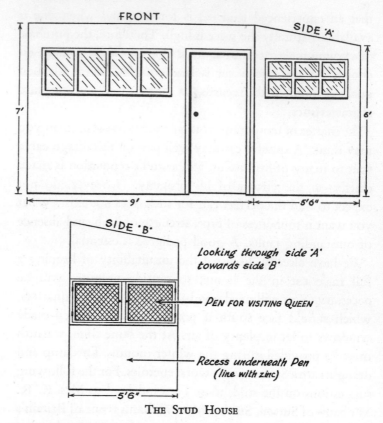

FRONT

SIDE 'A'

7'

6'

9'

5'6"

SIDE 'B'

Looking through side 'A' towards side 'B'

PEN FOR VISITING QUEEN

Recess underneath Pen (line with zinc)

5'6"

THE STUD HOUSE

house where it gets the longest hours of sunlight. The house I favour is the shape shown in the sketch; there is no wastage of warmth and it allows more freedom of movement.

"The house should be roughly 9 ft. long (7 ft. high at front, 6 ft. at back), with a depth back to front of 5–6 ft. When possible have windows in two sides; they give longer hours of sunlight within the house.

"Inside the house, a portion should be lined with zinc sheeting, 2 ft. to 2 ft. 6 ins. high and 2 ft. or more across the floor. The sanitary trays should be placed here. A pen for your visiting queens can be a fixture or movable, but it must be large enough to take her bed, toilet tray, and allow freedom of movement.

"Shelves should be fixed under both windows for your stud to sit and doze, or watch garden life. It is amazing to watch, from your own windows, a Siamese sitting on his shelf. His expression changes with his interest, and yet to the human eye there seems to be no movement.

"A stool or small chair on to which your stud can jump after mating a queen, or upon which he can sit and croon to her, is also a necessary part of the stud house.

"The stud sleeping box should be deep in winter and shallower in summer; the deeper box is warmer for winter months."

Adjoined to the stud house should be a long wired-in run. This is absolutely essential for exercise. Part of the run should consist of grass, but a good-sized patch of earth is also necessary for the cat's sanitary arrangements. Of course, the earth will be changed from time to time. Many breeders plant a tree trunk in the run so that the cat can sharpen its claws.

If you keep more than one stud cat, see that their houses are well away from each other, and if your queens are kept in outside houses then the stud should not be within sight of them either. This does not mean that the male Siamese is a ferocious animal. On the contrary, if given the right care, he is usually most gentle and affectionate. But if his house

51

is placed so that he can see the females all day long, it is only natural that he will become noisy and discontented.

Although the stud cat must, for the most part, live alone, never let him feel he is unloved. Be sure to visit him every day and spend as much time with him as possible. Always see that he is well groomed, talk to him, and pet him. You can even allow him a certain amount of freedom in the garden under strict supervision. It is not a good idea to allow a stud cat to roam at will, for he is bound to meet feline enemies on his travels. It is true that the male Siamese is usually a terrific fighter, so no doubt your pet will go unharmed. But even if you have no conscience for the other cats, there is always the possibility of infection and the grave danger of spreading germs throughout your cattery. And even if you are prepared to risk your own cats' health, it is hardly fair to visiting queens.

For your own females will be nowhere near sufficient for a virile male Siamese. Most studs are put at public service from the age of about twelve months, although during the first season they should only be used very sparingly. Later on, experience will show how many matings a stud requires; the average appears to be from two to three a week. The great point to remember is not to overwork your stud or the result may be sterility or sickly kittens.

Raw meat is an essential part of the stud cat's diet, and during the breeding season most fanciers feed about 6 oz. a day. But meat should not be the only food given, as balanced meals are most important. If you can spare an egg occasionally, this will be appreciated after mating. Parrish's Chemical Food is also useful, and yeast tablets act as a tonic to any cat. Always see that your pet has a bowl of water handy, for stud work will make him thirsty.

Every visiting queen should be examined thoroughly before penning, and if there is the slightest risk of contamination send her back at once. Of course, reputable breeders would never dream of sending an ill cat on any journey, let alone subject a colleague's cattery to infection. However, it is possible that a novice may err through ignorance. Cats rarely give in easily, and many a symptom may not be obvious to the inexperienced eye. Then, again, there is always the chance that a cat may pick up a germ on the journey.

Never put the female with your stud immediately, however loudly she may be calling. Few queens will mate at once, and if hurried might get spiteful and even injure the male. Put the queen in her own pen, and let the male run loose in his house so that they can gradually get to know each other through the wire partition. It is impossible to say exactly when the queen will allow the stud to mate her, but as a general guide it is safe to let her free when you hear her answering the male's croons.

Even so, maiden queens often prove difficult owing to nervousness. Experienced stud-owners usually manage to coax them quite easily with a little gentle petting, but the novice must be careful how he goes about this or he may get scratched or bitten.

After mating, the stud will jump on to the chair or stool that you have provided. He knows he must get away from the queen or she may fly at him in her excitement. The queen will probably scream or growl. She will certainly roll about and then start washing herself with great determination. Now is the time to remove the male. Never touch the female until she has quietened down, when you can put her back in the pen or bring her into the house in readiness for her return journey.

Although one mating is really quite sufficient, most stud-owners do give a second just to make sure. But do not leave the animals together to mate repeatedly, for this will only exhaust them.

6

Exhibiting Siamese Cats

BEFORE you can exhibit your cats at any show held under the rules of the Governing Council of the Cat Fancy, they must be entered in the Register kept by the Council. The only exceptions to this rule are kittens in litter classes, and household pets. In this Register is inserted the cat's name, date of birth, name of sire and dam and of grandsire and grandam.

Since December 1946 Siamese registrations have been kept separate from those of the other breeds, and forms for registering your pets can be obtained from the Assistant Secretary of the Governing Council, Mr. K. J. Aitken, 2, Commonfield Road, Banstead, Surrey. But should you wish to exhibit other cats in addition to Siamese, then these extra forms are supplied by the Secretary of the Governing Council, Mr. W. A. Hazeldine, 1 Roundwood Way, Banstead, Surrey.

When the form arrives, fill it up carefully in BLOCK LETTERS and send it back to Mr. Aitken, with a fee of 2*s*., at least four clear days before the closing date for entries. For each exhibit you will need a separate form, and for each you must send a separate fee. However, litters of not less than three kittens can be registered at a reduced charge of 1*s*. 6*d*. each, always provided that they are under six weeks old.

Owing to the thousands of names already registered, which cannot be repeated for twenty years, it is advisable to submit uncommon names. For example, such names as Felix, Queenie, Bluebell are almost bound to be recorded and should therefore be avoided. Numbers in figures or in words, such as Felix III or William the Fourth, will be disqualified, and so will names of living people, celebrated or otherwise. Finally, no name should exceed three words, including the prefix. Hyphenated words count as two words.

Practically all breeders adopt a prefix by which their cats are known. For example, anyone connected with the Cat Fancy even in the remotest way will immediately associate the Prestwick prefix as belonging to Mrs. Duncan Hindley's famous Siamese cats. Then there is the Doneraile prefix, which denotes Mrs. K. R. Williams' celebrated cats, the Southwood prefix indicating the cattery of Mrs. L. K. Sayers, to mention but a very few distinguished British breeders. As for individuality, you have only to glance at the titles under many of the photographs in this book to see what varied and original names can be chosen.

Once registered, no cat or kitten can have its name changed in any way. You will be sent a certificate of registration on which will be found the cat's number as recorded by the Governing Council of the Fancy. If the cat or kitten is sold, then transfer of ownership must also be registered before the animal can be shown again. This is done on a special pink transfer form, obtainable from Mr. Aitken at the address given previously. The form should be filled up and signed by the present owner, but it must also bear the signature of the last owner. A fee of 2s. must be sent back with the completed transfer form.

Once your cat is registered, the next step is to apply for a schedule and entry form. These are obtained from the show manager. Practically all the shows are organised by the various cat clubs, details of which will be given in the following chapter. Sometimes, however, a cat section is run in connection with a general livestock or horticultural exhibition, as, for example, the annual Sandy Championship Show. For particulars of forthcoming shows you should subscribe to *Fur and Feather*, which is the official organ of the Governing Council of the Cat Fancy (address: Watmoughs Ltd., Idle, Bradford, Yorks). Another magazine that breeders and exhibitors cannot afford to miss is *The Cat Fancy*, edited by Kit Wilson. This journal, which is devoted entirely to pedigree cats, is obtainable from The Loft, 18 South End, Kensington, London, W.8. Other periodicals for cat-lovers will be found listed at the end of this book.

Each club has its own show rules, and these, along with the Governing Council's rules, should be studied carefully before filling in the entry form. You must also decide in what classes to enter your pet. An open class is one in which all cats of any breed or variety of breeds can compete. A novice class is one confined to cats or kittens that have not won a first prize in any class at a show held under the Governing Council's rules. A radius class is limited to cats and kittens belonging to exhibitors residing within twenty-five miles of the show hall. Now here is the definition of classes as set down by the Siamese Cat Club for its annual Championship Show in 1949:

LIMIT CLASSES   For cats which have not won more than three first prizes at shows under rules of the G.C.C.F.

NOVICE CLASSES   For cats or kittens which have not won a first prize at shows under rules of the G.C.C.F.

JUNIOR CLASS   For cats under two years on day of Show.

SENIOR CLASS   For cats over two years on day of Show.

KITTEN CLASSES   Kittens over three and under nine months on the day of the Show.

BREEDERS' CLASSES   For cats or kittens bred by exhibitors.

LITTER CLASS   For three or more kittens of the same litter over six weeks and under three months old.

BRACE   For two cats or two kittens of either sex (i.e. two males or two females) belonging to the same exhibitor, each of which *must* be entered in at least one other class.

PAIR   For two cats or two kittens (one male, one female) belonging to the same exhibitor, each of which *must* be entered in at least one other class.

Brace exhibits are judged on individual merit, Pairs on their similarity to each other.

TEAM   For three exhibits, any sex or age, belonging to the same exhibitor, each of which *must* be entered in at least one other class.

> *Entries in brace, pair and team classes must be of one colour, i.e. all seal-pointed or blue-pointed.*

NOVICE EXHIBITORS   For exhibitors who have never won a prize, other than a special prize, under G.C. Rules.

RADIUS CLASSES   For cats or kittens belonging to exhibitors residing within twenty miles of Oxford Circus. Exhibits *must* be entered in at least one other class.

> *Blue-pointed and neuters are only eligible in their own classes unless specially stated.*

Now fill in the entry form in block letters and post it with the right amount of fees well before closing date.

To ensure success at shows, your cats must be in the best possible condition. Siamese only need ordinary common-sense grooming, and if this is carried out regularly they should look beautifully smooth and glossy on the day of the show. Use a rubber brush to get all the loose hairs out, and finish off by polishing with a piece of chamois leather. Always see that your pets are kept in clean surroundings, for unless their bedding is changed frequently no amount of brushing and combing will keep them free from fleas. Judges do not like to handle a cat with traces of fleas or ear-canker, even if it excels in show points.

If possible, get your cats used to being handled by strangers. This is especially important with Siamese, because some of them are very nervous. I can only think of one show where the exhibitors were allowed to take their cats up to the respective judges. The normal procedure in Britain is for each judge to have a steward, who takes the cat out of its pen and then places it on a small table ready for inspection.

Many cats are accustomed to the show pen from the time they are tiny kittens, and these usually quite enjoy the atmosphere. However, it must be admitted that a few Siamese (and, of course, other cats too) never seem happy in strange surroundings. The admiration of the public frightens them, and so does the enforced confinement. What is more, nervousness often makes such a cat spiteful and difficult to handle. Should one of your own cats be like this, I do entreat you not to show it. Let it remain at home in the garden or by the fire. After all, what are a few awards as compared to the happiness of your pet?

To take your cats to show you will need a good-sized hamper, as has already been described. Do not feed within two hours of departure, and when possible the last meal before the journey should consist of raw meat. Never, on any account, give milky food before travelling; just a drink of clean water. A soiled hamper is unpleasant both for yourself and the cat.

On arrival, all cats are examined by the show's veterinary surgeon. If an animal is unwell or has the slightest symptoms of infection, then the vet has full authority to order its immediate removal from the hall. This is only fair to the other exhibits.

But once your cats are passed you take them into the hall and prepare to pen them. Having found their cages, it is wise to clean these out with a little methylated spirit, which you should take with you. Most breeders also disinfect the pens with Sanitas or Dettol. When penning, swab each cat's mouth out with a piece of cotton wool soaked in diluted T.C.P. (one part T.C.P. to five or six parts water). T.C.P. is perfectly safe to give internally; in fact, it is a very useful antidote for worms.

Such precautions may seem unnecessary, and, indeed, show managers do everything in their power to eliminate the danger of infection. All the same, when so many animals are collected together there is bound to be some risk. You can greatly reduce this yourself by never showing a cat that is not in perfect health. Far better forfeit an entrance fee than expose your colleagues' pets to infection. A most important rule of the Governing Council which is printed on every show entry form reads as follows:

"No exhibitor shall exhibit a cat or kitten which to his or her knowledge has, at the date of the show, been exposed to any infectious or contagious illness within the period of twenty-one days prior to the date of the show, and no cat or kitten may be exhibited if the exhibitor has had any such illness in his or her cattery during that period. Any exhibitor who, in the opinion of the Council, shall have made a false declaration in respect of the above will be liable to severe penalties."

After sending in your entry form, you should have received a small tally (or tallies) bearing the same number as that of your cat's pen. Tie this round your pet's neck with white (not coloured) tape before penning. Do *not* decorate the cage in any way until after the judging is over. No cushions are allowed inside the pen, but a small white blanket without markings is permissible for the cat's comfort. This should be folded quite flat. You will also need to take a small sanitary tray with you, but peat moss litter is provided by the show management. Do not feed your cat until after the judging, although drinking water should not be withheld.

When the judging begins, you will be asked to leave the hall, although exhibitors are allowed to watch from the gallery if they wish to do so. Of course, all judges have their own methods, but one thing you may be certain of: absolute fairness is assured. Cats' names never appear in the judges' books, their anonymity being preserved by numbers. After the assessment of each class the judge sends a slip containing the winning number to the Secretary's table, from where notices of the awards are placed on a board for all to see.

Awards are numerous and vary from money prizes and trophies to rosettes, travelling hampers, and subscriptions to cat magazines. Quite apart from the general run of prizes, special awards are often made for cats—such as a Siamese with the best whip tail, the cat in best condition, easiest to handle, and so on.

To become a full champion, a cat must win three championship certificates under three different judges. The Governing Council of the Cat Fancy decides on the number of championship certificates to be offered for each variety of cat during the show season, and at what shows they shall be granted. To compete for a championship certificate, a cat must have won a first prize in its class at that particular show. Championship certificates are awarded to adult cats only,

XXII. Royette Remus, owned by Mrs. Smith of Cheshire, best Neuter at the
Siamese Cat Club Championship Show at Lime Grove Hall, Shepherd's Bush,
London.

XXIII. Mystic Dreamer, father of the famous prizewinning cat Lindale Simon Pie and holder of many awards himself. He is owned by Mrs. G. E. Matthes of Lough-borough, Leics.

kittens being allowed only to compete in their own classes. When all the judging is completed, voting takes place for "Best Cat in the Show". Some show managements appoint a special panel of judges to decide this important matter; at other shows all the judges give an opinion, with a referee judge to give the casting vote in the case of two cats tying for the coveted award. Needless to say, this referee judge is always a supreme authority.

Once the general public is admitted, exhibitors can go to their respective cats and remain by their pens for the rest of the day. It is then permissible to feed your pets and make them look as attractive as you please. If you like, you can also decorate their cages. What you must not do is take them home until the show closes, unless, of course, you have special permission to do so. If you sell a cat or kitten at the show, it can usually be handed over to its new owner at 4 p.m.

Naturally, it is extremely gratifying for one's cats to become prize-winners. But should you see no award cards on their pens, do take it in a sporting manner. To go around the hall complaining that a cat has always won at other shows and would have done this time only . . . will certainly not make for popularity with your fellow breeders. Even if it is true that your pet has done better on previous occasions, he (or she) may be a little "off colour" on this particular day. Condition counts for a great deal with judges.

But if you are in any real doubt as to your cat's success, why not have a word with the judge about it? Go to him at a quiet moment and ask for his advice regarding your pet's show qualities. No judge will mind explaining a cat's faults, and even offer help regarding improvement, provided, of course, that you do not question his decision. Judges are noted for their kindness to novice breeders. After all, they had to begin.

When the show is over, swab out your cat's mouth again with diluted T.C.P., then get it home as soon as possible. Give it a good meal, and if you can spare a few drops of whisky or brandy, this will help to keep out chills. Rubbing the fur over with Sanitas or Dettol is also a wise precaution. And if other cats are kept, then try to isolate the one which has visited the show for at least a week.

7

Should You Join a Cat Club?

WHETHER you keep Siamese cats for breeding and exhibition purposes or just as household pets, it will certainly pay you to join one of the specialist clubs catering exclusively for this breed. As a pet-owner, you will get much help and information about your hobby. As an exhibitor, you will be able to compete for the cups, and other attractive prizes, which these clubs offer to members at all the important shows.

Most fanciers also like to join a district club, so that they can meet and exchange views with other cat-lovers in their neighbourhood. Many of these local cat clubs hold social functions, arrange debates and lectures on matters of feline interest, and so on.

But before discussing the full benefits to be derived from joining a cat club, it might be interesting to recall how such organisations came into existence. They actually date back to the very first Cat Show held at the Crystal Palace in 1871. This show was sponsored by Harrison Weir, well known in his day as an artist and great animal-lover. He wished that the public might see how beautiful a well-cared-for cat could look. "Why", he wrote, "should not the cat that sits purring in front of us before the fire be an object of interest, and be selected for its colour, markings, and form?"

However, that first Crystal Palace Cat Show was very different from exhibitions of the present day. Listen to Harrison Weir again: "There lay the cats in their pens, reclining on crimson cushions, making no sound save now and then a homely purring, as from time to time they lapped the nice new milk provided for them."

One great difference between those very early shows and those we know to-day was that pedigree did not seem to matter. Also the classes were defined quite differently at that time. For the most part, exhibits consisted of short-haired cats, the long-hairs, or Angoras, as they were usually called, being greatly in the minority. However, the Crystal Palace venture was a great success and became a much-looked-forward-to annual event.

Gradually other cat shows followed suit, many of them continuing over a period of two or three days. Indeed, by the summer of 1887, so popular had such shows become that at a large four-day exhibition a number of fanciers got together and planned to form a club. And so it was that the National Cat Club came into existence, with Harrison Weir as its first President.

During the years that followed, the National Cat Club

served the same purpose as the Governing Council of the Cat Fancy does to-day. It kept the official register, and fixed a standard of points for each variety of cat. It issued championship certificates, and in 1893 published the first stud book of cats. In the course of time the President, Harrison Weir, was succeeded by the famous cat artist, Louis Wain.

Until 1898 there was no serious opposition. Then, as a result of a rift in membership, the Cat Club, with Lady Marcus Beresford as President, was formed. This new club caused a great deal of confusion in the Fancy, one of the chief difficulties being that it persisted in keeping yet another official register of cats. Meanwhile, a number of smaller clubs were founded, some, like the Siamese Cat Club, to cater for a particular breed, others, such as the Midland Counties Cat Club and the Southern Counties Cat Club, to provide for feline interests in particular districts.

Now, while some of these societies were loyal to the National Cat Club, others were swayed by the rival organisation, and although the Cat Club came to an end in 1904, unfortunately its influence persisted. Even a special Cat Fancier Association which was formed to try to clear up the trouble was not very successful. So in 1910 a meeting was called and the Governing Council of the Cat Fancy came into existence, with the object of controlling the interests of the Cat Fancy in much the same way as the Kennel Club does for dog-breeders.

The Governing Council consists of delegates sent from all the cat clubs, each club having the right to choose its own delegate. Because the National Cat Club resigned its position of authority in favour of the Governing Council, it was given the right to send a larger number of delegates than the other clubs, and so it has four representatives to-day.

And now for some details of the various clubs and what they set out to accomplish. Since this book is written chiefly for owners and would-be owners of Siamese cats, the specialist clubs for this breed must come first. The Siamese Cat Club, which is presided over by Compton Mackenzie, was founded in 1901 and is the largest specialist cat club in Europe, probably in the world. Objects of the club are:

1 To promote the pure breeding of Siamese cats, and to safeguard and encourage fair dealing and kind treatment to all cats.
2 To draw up standards of points for Siamese cats and to distribute the same amongst members.
3 To hold and support shows for the exhibition of Siamese cats.
4 To improve the classification of, and, if necessary, the guaranteeing of classes for Siamese cats at shows supported by the club.
5 To select specialist judges to make the awards at such shows.
6 To support any body or bodies whose objects include the promotion of the welfare or pure breeding of the feline species.

Membership of the Siamese Cat Club is open to anyone interested in the breed, but every candidate *must* be proposed and seconded by a member of the Club. Advice is gladly given to any member, whether they breed Siamese cats, own just one cat, or wish to have one. The Club also runs a comprehensive and very interesting monthly news-sheet.

The following list will give some idea of the many beautiful challenge cups and trophies offered by the Siamese Cat Club to its members for competition at the various cat shows each year[1]:

SANCHO (PRESIDENT'S CUP), for the best adult male or female cat.

The BREEDERS' CUP, for the best male or female cat bred by an exhibitor.

The NOVICE CUP, for best novice, male or female.

The KITTEN CUP, for the best kitten, male or female.

The Champion SIMPLE BOWL, for the most typical-headed Siamese in adult male or female classes.

The MARY ROBINSON TROPHY, for the best pair, male and female adults.

The ORIENTAL TROPHY, for the best team, comprising not less than three.

The BRITANNIA CUP, for the best brood queen: judged by progeny in show.

The Ch. SIMZO CUP, for the best stud cat: judged by progeny in show.

The BLUEBOI CUP, for best blue-pointed kitten.

The SHUVELANG TROPHY, for best kitten pair, male and female.

The GRATEFUL CUP, for best litter.

The NOVICE KITTEN CUP, for best novice kitten, male or female.

[1] New ruling, 1951. No kitten under the age of eight weeks may be sold at the club show.

The BREEDERS' KITTEN CUP, for best kitten, male or female.

The PRESTWICK CUP, for best and deepest blue eyes in male or female adult.

The Ch. PRESTWICK PERAK CUP, for best veteran over 5 years.

The SABIA OF CADEMUIR TROPHY, for best veteran over five years of opposite sex to the winner of the Ch. Prestwick Perak Cup.

The DARLANDS CHALLENGE PLATE, for best neuter over one year.

The SHUVELITA REMEMBRANCE CUP, for adult female over two years of age with lightest cream coat, densest seal points, most typical shape.

SILVER SPECIAL, for best slanting eyes (Oriental) in adult male or female.

The NUNKIE CUP, for the most slanting (Oriental) eyes (irrespective of colour) in adults.

The LONGHAM CUP, for best brace of kittens (two males or two females).

The D.S.M. CUP, for the finest and closest texture of coat in adult male cat.

The CORVINE CUP, for best type in male kittens.

The FITZWILLIAM TROPHY, for the stud cat whose kittens score most points at the Siamese Cat Club Show.

The Ch. MORGAN LE FAY TROPHY, to be won outright by the first member to breed both the best male and the best female in the same year's show.

The ASHURSTWOOD CUP, to be offered annually at

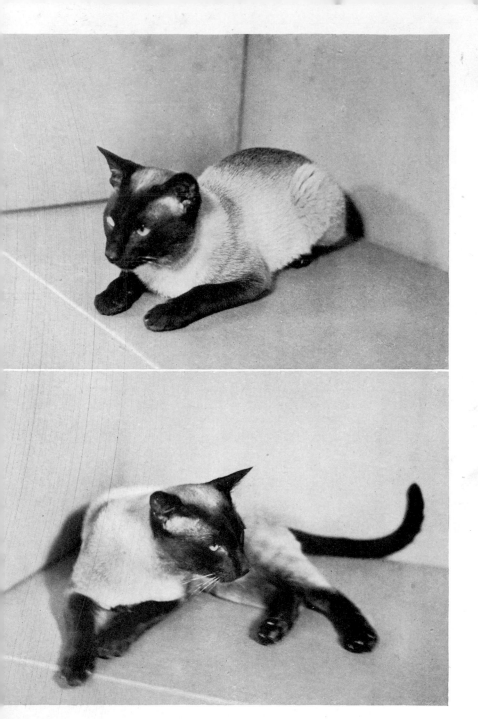

XXIV, XXV.   Champion Hillcross Song, bred by Mrs. Towe and owned by Mrs. Druce of Cyprus. Winner of the open male adult class at the Siamese Cat Club's Championship Show in 1949. See page 99.

XXVI.   Ch. Inwood Shadow, holder of four championships, 23 Firsts and many other awards. Note the points—ears large and pricked, wide at the base, and eyes slanting towards the nose. Born in 1947, Shadow was bred by her owner Mrs. A. S. McGregor, of Nettlestead, near Maidstone, and has been widely acclaimed as the best Siamese Female bred in this country since the war.

Leicester Mercury

XXVII. Lindale Simon Pie with his owner, Mrs. Linda Parker, of Cropstone, Leicester. To date Simon Pie holds 6 silver cups, 19 Firsts and silver and bronze medals. See page 99.

XXVIII.   Mr. Michael Joseph with his two cats, Binks and Jemima Gray. Jemima Gray is the Siamese.

XXIX.   Vivien Leigh with her Siamese cat, New, taken during the making of *Anna Karenina*.

the Club Show to the member whose cats, bred by the exhibitor, are awarded most points.

The PERCIVAL CUP, for the exhibitor whose adult cats score the highest number of points in open classes during the show season. (A small replica to be given each year to the winner.)

The SHAKESPEARE CUP, for the exhibitor whose kittens score the highest number of points in open classes during the show season. (A small replica to be given each year to the winner.)

The LLOYD LEWIS MEMORIAL CUP, for the breeder of the adult cat that has scored the highest number of points during the show season at championship shows. (A small replica to be given each year to the winner.)

The WHITE WALTHAM CUP, for the best female adult (restricted to the owners of one queen only).

The BEDALE CUP, for a female cat which is easy to handle and in perfect condition, irrespective of show points.

The BURKE TROPHY, for the best wedge-shaped head.

The SOUTH LAWN SASHA CUP, for best female adult.

The LADY KATHLEEN CURZON-HERRICK TROPHY, for the best veteran (either sex).

The ANGUS ROMNEY TROPHY, for the adult male with palest body colour, over four years.

The PHYL WADE MEMORIAL CUP, for best adult male, kitten or neuter that is in the best condition and easiest to handle, irrespective of show points.

The TOSTOCK CUP, for the finest and closest texture of coat in kittens.

The d'OLLONE SIAMESE CUP, for the finest descendant of a Bedale cat, male or female.

The annual subscription to the Siamese Cat Club is 5s. and entrance fee £1 1s. Life Membership, £5 5s.

Fuller details can be obtained from the Hon. Secretary, Mrs. E. Hart, Tye Cottage, Frog Grove Lane, Wood Street, Guildford, Surrey.

THE SIAMESE CAT SOCIETY OF THE BRITISH EMPIRE

The Siamese Cat Society of the British Empire has Michael Joseph for its President and is open to all who are interested in Siamese cats, whether they are breeders, owners of neuters or of just one pet. Special trophies offered to members throughout the season include:

The LITAMAN CUP, for the best veteran cat over four years.

The CHEPPING BLUE EYES GIFT, for the best blue eyes in adult female cat.

The PRESIDENT'S CUP, for the best Siamese stud.

The HENRY GRAY CUP, for the best adult female.

The SIMOUR BOWL, for the best cat and/or kitten, male or female, winning most points in open classes at championship shows under one ownership.

The RAG TAG CUP, for the best Siamese brood queen.

The FLEET TROPHY, for the best blue-pointed adult male bred by exhibitor; slanting eyes essential.

The annual subscription is 5s. Life membership, £3 3s.

Hon. Secretary: Miss Beckett, Esher, Uffington Road, Willesden, London, N.W.10.

THE BLUE-POINTED SIAMESE CAT CLUB is an exclusive society for owners of blue-points, and is open for membership to all those interested, whether for breeding or pets. This Club also offers many attractive awards to its members during the show season. Annual subscription, 5s., with an entrance fee of 10s. Life membership, £3 3s.

Hon. Secretary: Mr. W. Lamb, Twylands, Grange Hill, Halesowen, Birmingham.

Although the NATIONAL CAT CLUB caters for all breeds of cat, it has very many Siamese owners among its large membership. A few privileges to be enjoyed by members are:

1 Numerous challenge trophies and many special prizes confined to members at the club's annual championship show.
2 Smaller entry fee at the club show.
3 Special members' classes, with attractive money prizes.
4 Special members' classes at all the big shows.
5 Special prizes, confined to members, at all the big shows.

Annual subscription to this club is £1 1s. Life membership, £10 10s.

Hon. Secretary: Mrs. Brunton, Marlpost Farm, Southwater, Horsham, Sussex.

THE SOUTHERN COUNTIES CAT CLUB was founded in 1904, and ranks second in status to the National Cat Club, having the right of permanently returning two members to the Governing Council of the Cat Fancy. It holds an annual show in London, where handsome silver championship trophies are offered. Liberal support is also given to all other shows. This Club is open to all cat-lovers. Hon. Secretary is Mrs. K. R. Williams, the well-known judge and one of our foremost Siamese cat-breeders.

The annual subscription is 7s. 6d., with an entrance fee of 2s. 6d. Life membership, £5 5s.

Hon. Secretary: Mrs. K. R. Williams, 92 Chiltern Road, Sutton, Surrey.

THE KENSINGTON KITTEN AND NEUTER CAT CLUB has for its President Miss Rachel Ferguson, and Vice-President, Michael Joseph. It is a club which caters for all breeders, as well as the owners of just one cat, and it also gives a hearty welcome to associate (non-showing) members. Over thirty cups are offered for competition at the Club's annual show, and cups and other attractive prizes are offered at all shows throughout the season. The Club arranges social gatherings for members and their friends for debates, discussions, and lectures on cats.

The annual subscription is 5s. for full membership; associate (non-showing) membership 3s. 6d., which includes admission to the Club show. Life membership, £3 3s.

Hon. Secretary: Mr. F. B. Williams, 92 Chiltern Road, Sutton, Surrey.

THE CROYDON CAT CLUB has a membership of over 300. It is open to all, and its objects are to promote the breeding and exhibition of cats, to assist cat-fanciers in all

matters pertaining to their hobby, and to encourage the
public to take an active interest in the care and protection of
cats. Numerous trophies and other special awards are offered
to members at the Club's annual championship show, and
classes are guaranteed for members at all other shows. The
Club also circulates its own news-sheet to members.

The annual subscription is 5s. There is no entrance fee.
Life membership, £3 3s.

Hon. Secretary: Mrs. E. Towe, 239 Hillcross Avenue,
Morden, Surrey.

Some other clubs open to Siamese cat owners include the
following:

HERTFORDSHIRE AND MIDDLESEX CAT CLUB.
All breeds. Annual subscription, 5s. Hon. Secretary: Mrs.
Parker, 31 Hempstead Road, King's Langley, Herts.

LANCASHIRE AND NORTH-WESTERN
COUNTIES CAT CLUB. All breeds. Annual subscription,
5s. Hon. Secretary: Mrs. Culley, 65 Westbourne Park,
Urmston, Lancs.

MIDLAND COUNTIES CAT CLUB. All breeds.
Annual subscription, 5s. Entrance fee, 2s. 6d. Hon. Secretary:
Mrs. O. M. Lamb, Twylands, Grange Hill, Halesowen,
Birmingham.

NOTTS AND DERBY CAT CLUB. All breeds.
Annual subscription, 5s. Entrance fee, 2s. 6d. Hon. Secretary:
Mr. J. F. Barker, Sylvan House, 49 Church Street, Ilkeston,
Derbyshire.

SCOTTISH CAT CLUB. All breeds. Annual subscription,

7s. 6d. Hon. Secretary: Mrs. F. M. Richardson, 21 Herriet Street, Glasgow, S.1.

SHORT-HAIRED CAT SOCIETY OF GREAT BRITAIN. All the short-haired breeds. Annual subscription, 5s. Hon. Secretary: Mrs. E. Towe, 239 Hillcross Avenue, Morden, Surrey.

SOUTHSEA CAT CLUB. All breeds. Annual subscription, 5s. Entrance fee, 3s. 6d. Chairman: Mrs. Cook-Radmore, Seven Oaks, Cowplain, Hants.

SOUTH-WESTERN COUNTIES CAT CLUB. All breeds. Annual subscription, 7s. 6d. No entrance fee. Hon. Secretary: Miss Cathcart, Trelystan, Dunstone Park, Paignton, Devon.

YORKSHIRE CAT CLUB. All breeds. Hon. Secretary: J. Jenkinson, 2 Russell Street, Bingley.

8

Some Common Ailments

WHEN many of my friends first heard that I had a Siamese cat, they shook their heads and told me I would never rear him. I believe it is a fallacy that Siamese cats are especially delicate, although no doubt they were when first imported. Some people may be unfortunate enough to buy a fragile kitten, but that is just bad luck. They might, surely, have the same misfortune with a Persian cat or one of any other breed.

As long as your Siamese kitten comes from healthy stock, is cared for, and fed correctly, it should seldom ail. Personally, I have had far less trouble with Cæsar regarding illness than with many other pets, and as I have never been without at least one cat or dog, I can speak from some experience.

However, I do feel that perhaps some people confine Siamese cats too much. These remarks do not refer to breeders, for they are specialists, and for the most part house their cats under the best possible conditions. But I have occasionally met people who, because they have paid five or six guineas for a pet, think more of its monetary value than of the cat's health, and are afraid to let it out in the sunshine in case it may be stolen.

If you have a garden, do allow your pet as much freedom as it wishes, although if you live on a main road it may be advisable to wire the garden in. You will not want to risk your Siamese being run over.

Few cats will venture out in bad weather, but, strangely enough, many Siamese do not seem to mind the rain. Cæsar is so accustomed to complete freedom that he loudly registers protest when I refuse to open the door for him during a heavy shower. All the same, one cannot be too careful, for a drenching can set up all kinds of serious complaints.

This book does not set out to describe the treatment of illness in full detail. There are better qualified people to do that than myself. Whenever my own pets are ill, I call the vet immediately, and even if my suspicions prove a false alarm, I consider the fee well spent. So all I propose to do here is to set down some of the minor ailments which do, as a rule, respond satisfactorily to home treatment, and list a few of the more complicated illnesses so that you may understand the symptoms and have a few remedies at hand until the vet arrives.

The great point to remember about all cats is that they rarely let you know when they are unwell. Probably this is because they are seldom ill, or, more likely, it is owing to their independent natures. Once they become seriously

XXX.   Eebou, beloved pet of Olivia Manning. See page 104.

XXXI.   Slug, a Seal-pointed Siamese, owned by Mrs. J. Kohlus of East Rockaway, awaits the Judges' decision at the Long Island Cat Show in Hempstead. Above her hang the ribbons she won previously.

ill, however, they give in very easily, and unless you do act quickly the disease may prove fatal.

A rise in temperature is always a danger sign. The normal temperature of a cat is 101·4, or practically 101½°, and for the most accurate reading should be taken in the rectum. Use an ordinary half-minute thermometer and get someone to hold the cat. Shake the mercury down to 98°, smear the point well with vaseline and very gently insert it for about 1½ ins. into the cat's rectum. Leave it there for about a minute.

MINOR AILMENTS

THE COMMON COLD A cat with a slight chill does not usually go off its food, and this is one very clear way of knowing whether the trouble is just a cold or symptom of a more serious illness. The common cold takes much the same form with cats as it does with humans, i.e. frequent sneezing, watery discharge from the eyes and nostrils, and often a sore throat. As a rule, there is little or no temperature, and as long as you take reasonable care of your pet the trouble should soon clear up. Feed on raw meat if possible, but if the throat is sore, then lightly steamed fish or something in the nature of Brand's Beef Essence may be more acceptable. An egg beaten up in Sherley's Lactol also makes a nourishing invalid meal. Drinking water should always be available.

Keep the cat warm—in one room for preference. If your pet is allowed to run in and out, a fresh chill may develop, and, should this turn to pneumonia, may be very serious indeed. Regarding medicines, a small dose of milk of magnesia prevents constipation. Or yeast tablets answer the same purpose and also act as a tonic. Most Siamese love yeast and will eat the tablets like sweets, so there should be no difficulty over persuading your pet to take them. I would also mix homœopathic aconite 3X in the cat's food: two pillules for an adult cat, one for a kitten. My own vet is a firm believer in homœopathic preparations for feline complaints, and as I have used them with tremendous success both for animals and humans, naturally I agree with him.

CONSTIPATION This is chiefly caused through wrong diet, although it may occur through lack of exercise, hair-ball, or some more serious complaint. If the cat is lively-spirited, then it is safe to assume that diet or lack of exercise is the fault and treat accordingly. If my cat seems constipated, I give him a teaspoonful of pure olive oil, or mix two homœopathic nux vomica pills (3X potency) in his food. Nux is extremely mild and absolutely harmless. As a rule, it will clear up the trouble in no time. Kittens should have a smaller dose.

Yeast tablets given daily keep the organs in good working order, as does lightly boiled liver occasionally. Milk also has a laxative effect. In obstinate cases, medicinal paraffin oil or milk of magnesia may be given quite safely; about a teaspoonful is usually sufficient for an adult cat. Never give castor oil or any other strong aperient to a cat, excepting under veterinary guidance.

INDIGESTION This is caused by irregular or wrong feeding; also lack of exercise. Symptoms are poor appetite, excessive thirst, and continual yawning. Sometimes there is restlessness and vomiting after food. Discontinue milky foods and feed primarily on minced raw meat. A small dose of milk of magnesia should be given twice daily, or homœopathic nux vomica 3X can be mixed with the food. See that your pet has sufficient exercise, and avoid overloading its stomach. Better give smaller meals at more frequent intervals than occasional very large ones.

HAIR-BALL Siamese cats are not subject to hair-ball in the stomach as are the long-haired types, but during the moulting season there is always the danger of this trouble. You can do a great deal to prevent it by making sure your cat is properly groomed. Daily brushing and combing helps to remove the loose hairs, which otherwise may accumulate in the cat's stomach when it licks itself. Also see that your pet has plenty of grass, for this encourages the vomiting of hair-ball. A small knob of margarine or a dose of olive oil is also very beneficial.

DIARRHŒA There are many causes of this complaint, worms and undigested food being among the most usual. With tiny kittens diarrhœa is sometimes caused by the change of food when weaning, but it can also be a symptom of more serious illnesses and occurs frequently in distemper. Assuming that the trouble is of a minor nature, the diarrhœa can be stopped with carbonate of bismuth. For a kitten, give as much as will cover a sixpence, for a cat a larger dose, and mix this with the food three times a day. Kaolin is an alternative remedy in such cases, and this should be given after meals. Discontinue the treatment after a few days and watch results. If there is a recurrence, then consult a vet, for to effect a permanent cure it is essential to get at the cause. In all cases of diarrhœa the cat's diet must be watched carefully. Feed on raw meat as far as possible and cut out all milky foods. Arrowroot or cornflour made with water usually proves helpful, and barley water makes a good drink.

OFFENSIVE BREATH This again can come from many reasons, the most frequent being worms, bad teeth, or indigestion. Treatment for worms will be discussed shortly; indigestion has been dealt with. A cat's teeth should always be examined periodically, and any signs of tartar removed by a vet. Elderly cats sometimes have a loose tooth, and this causes bad breath. Sweetened, sloppy, and starchy food will do much to ruin a cat's teeth, whereas correct diet will preserve them.

PARASITES

WORMS Most kittens are troubled with worms, and as long as your pet is in good health otherwise, this need not alarm you unduly. There are a number of proprietary worm medicines on the market; some of these are excellent, others not so good. The fact remains that hundreds of kittens die from indiscriminate worming, and personally I would not give a vermifuge to any cat unless under the advice of a good vet or animal clinic.

Usually a wormy cat is painfully thin, despite a ravenous appetite. Or it may be terribly hungry one day and completely off its food the next. Other symptoms are a harsh and "staring" coat and/or a distended stomach. Sometimes a cough is noticeable, and, with kittens, a persistent form of diarrhœa.

Round-worms particularly infest kittens and young cats. They form in large clusters in the intestines, from where they sometimes crawl into the stomach and are vomited up. Tape-worms grow long and ribbon-like, and often segments are passed with the cat's motion. These parasites usually affect older cats.

Both round- and tape-worms will sap a cat's vitality if it is in a poor state of health. Otherwise they usually cause little trouble. Therefore, unless I knew for certain that my cat had worms, I would concentrate on building up his powers of resistance with plenty of good food, a course of yeast tablets, and an occasional dose of olive oil. Also, about once a week I would give him a small quantity of T.C.P. mixed with milk or water (about a teaspoonful of T.C.P. to five of water).

It is interesting to observe that cats fed entirely on fresh raw meat rarely suffer from worms, which only goes to prove that faulty diet has a good deal to do with the trouble.

FLEAS Even the most carefully-groomed cat will harbour an occasional flea during the warm weather. This is soon disposed of by combing with a fine steel comb dipped into a solution of diluted Dettol or Milton. The flea-infested cat, however, is a more serious problem. Quite apart from the unpleasantness of having an animal in this condition around you, fleas cause a great deal of irritation to the cat. Also, they act as intermediate hosts for tape-worm.

There are a number of insect powders on the market, but be sure not to use one containing D.D.T., for this may prove fatal if the animal licks itself. A powder containing pyrethrum is about your best choice, for this is extremely effective and perfectly harmless to the cat. Dust the powder well into the cat's fur, and then rub the whole body gently with your finger-tips. Next put the cat in a linen bag, or wrap it in a clean white sheet with only the head protruding. Hold your pet in this position for ten or fifteen minutes and then brush out the remainder of the powder. You will be surprised at the number of fleas that remain in the bag.

This treatment should be repeated at seven- or ten-day intervals. However, two applications are usually sufficient. But do be sure to keep the cat's bedding clean. And if your pet is fond of playing in dusty cupboards and corners, have these scrubbed out. Such spots are favourite breeding places for fleas.

LICE Siamese cats are not usually troubled with lice, as these pests are more prone to attack the long-haired varieties. Indications of lice are a dull and sticky coat with much scratching on the part of the cat. The most effective treatment is to bathe the cat in warm water to which a disinfectant, such as Dettol or Milton, has been added, or you can ask your vet to recommend a suitable shampoo. Combing the coat thoroughly with a solution of vinegar and water (one part vinegar to two parts water) also produces good results. Use a fine steel comb for the purpose.

TICKS These parasites are not likely to worry the town cat, but your Siamese living in the country is liable to pick up a tick, especially if it has access to fields where sheep have been grazing. Although ticks are seldom noticed just at first, they are extremely dangerous. In the early stages they look like small warts. They attach themselves to their victim, bury their heads in the animal's skin and suck the blood, thus sapping the cat's energy. As the tick's body fills with blood so it swells out and becomes greyish-blue in colour. At this stage it is very easy to distinguish, but difficult to remove, for if the head is not completely dislodged the pest will only grow again. To make the tick release its hold, place a drop of turpentine at the point where the head is buried, then remove the tick with a pair of tweezers.

EAR-CANKER There are various forms of ear-canker, but the most usual is caused by a parasite which breeds in the ear and sets up intense irritation. The complaint is highly contagious, and although it is fairly easy to cure in the early stages, when neglected it can be a long and difficult business.

A cat suffering from canker will shake its head frequently and scratch inside the ear, which becomes very sensitive to touch and often feels burning hot. Again, the cat may hang its head on one side or rub it against the furniture in an effort to ease the irritation. Closer examination of the ear will disclose a brownish discharge, under which a number of tiny insects will be seen moving about.

To clear up the trouble, pour a little warm olive oil into the cat's ear and leave for about ten minutes. Meanwhile, gently massage the base of the ear to make quite sure the oil reaches all the crevices. Now carefully remove the crusts with a piece of cotton-wool wrapped round the end of an orange-stick. Be sure to do this very gently or you may make the ear bleed. When all the dirt has been removed, dust in a little canker powder or boric acid powder. Repeat the treatment daily until the ears look perfectly clean.

In very serious cases of ear-canker the parasites appear

to cause giddiness. The cat is unable to walk straight; it staggers along for a yard or so and then falls on its side. No sooner does it get up than it staggers and falls again. Other alarming symptoms are abscesses and deafness. Needless to say, such long-standing neglect should be dealt with by a veterinary surgeon.

SKIN DISEASES

DANDRUFF A good many cats are troubled with dandruff, which is due to a dry form of eczema. Try rubbing just a very little olive oil into your pet's skin before brushing. This treatment, combined with a change of diet and a course of yeast tablets, should soon effect a cure.

ECZEMA Not many Siamese cats are troubled with eczema, but when it does occur a permanent cure is often difficult, for the disease is always liable to break out afresh during the warm weather. Little is known of the actual cause, but most authorities consider it is due to impure blood, usually the result of injudicious or over-feeding.

Eczema is *not* contagious. It may break out either in a dry, scaly form or as moist eczema, with a rash that is continually discharging. For treatment, a soothing lotion should be applied as prescribed by your veterinary surgeon, or you can try bathing with boracic crystals dissolved in warm water (a teaspoonful of crystals to a pint of water); then gently dry with a piece of soft, clean rag. This should reduce the inflammation. In severe cases it is advisable to make a wide cardboard collar and place it round the cat's neck. This will prevent your pet from licking the affected parts and so give them a chance to heal.

Special attention should always be given to diet. If a cat has been fed exclusively on fish, it may be a good idea to change over to a meat diet. If meat has been the sole item of diet, then try fish for a short while. A course of yeast tablets should prove extremely beneficial, and care must always be taken to guard against constipation.

RINGWORM Ringworm is not often found in cats, although they do sometimes contract it from infected rats and mice, or from lying in straw where cows have been.

This highly infectious disease is due to a fungus. There are two different types—"honeycomb" ringworm and "grey" ringworm. It is the latter kind which is most common to cats.

Early symptoms may be patches of hair coming out from round the cat's head or neck, or perhaps there will be a roughness of skin with dry, grey scales rather like dandruff in appearance. On closer inspection, you may find a raised circular patch of bare skin, although sometimes the areas are irregular, owing to the diseased patches running into each other.

Ringworm can certainly be cured, but whenever it is suspected it is absolutely essential to seek veterinary advice. The disease spreads very rapidly and is highly contagious both to other animals and to human beings.

MANGE Cats which are well cared for are rarely attacked by mange, unless this foul disease is passed on by a prowling fellow sufferer. Again there are two varieties—sarcoptic mange and follicular mange. The former is more common to cats. Although in the advanced stages this often looks worse than follicular mange, usually it is the easier type to cure. Both kinds are due to parasites.

Sarcoptic mange generally appears on the head and neck, and if taken early enough, will not spread to other parts of the body. Symptoms are the cat's repeated scratching of the affected parts owing to the tremendous irritation. The hair comes off in patches and tiny pimples are usually to be seen on the bare skin. Continued scratching causes these to break; scabs form, becoming scaly and crusted with blood.

Veterinary advice should be sought immediately mange is suspected, and dressings carried out unremittingly as prescribed. You will have to keep the cat at home, for no vet dare risk boarding a cat with mange: it is too infectious for other animals which may be at the surgery. If you keep other pets yourself, then isolate the infected animal. Once cured, all bedding must be burnt and surroundings thoroughly disinfected.

Follicular mange begins with small, scaly patches, which soon spread rapidly over the whole body. The skin takes on a greyish tint and becomes hard and wrinkled-looking. Owing to the poisons in the system, the cat becomes exceedingly depressed, so, besides following a very strict routine regarding dressings, you will have to see that your pet's strength is built up with good but not starchy food. With patience, both types of mange can normally be cured in a matter of three or four weeks.

FITS Fits are very rare in cats, but they do have them occasionally. Kittens are especially susceptible when cutting their second teeth or if suffering from worms. Symptoms vary.

The animal may seem quite well one minute, then suddenly falls over on its side, kicking violently and perhaps foaming at the mouth. In other cases the kitten rushes about, knocking into furniture and anything else within its reach. Or, again, it may stand quite still, crying hysterically as if in pain.

In all cases of fits, the vet is the best person to advise on treatment. All you should do is try to calm the cat until he arrives. Never touch a cat while in a fit or you may get scratched or bitten badly. Not that such bites are harmful, but they are very far from pleasant. The best way of tackling the problem is to throw a large, thick cloth or blanket over your pet so that you can pick it up safely. Then place it in a basket and close the lid down. Leave the basket in a darkened room until the vet arrives. If the cat quietens down meanwhile, you can let it out of the basket, but get the vet to examine it just the same.

BLADDER TROUBLE   Male cats, especially neuters, sometimes get cystitis or gravel in the bladder. Symptoms are a general listlessness, refusal to take food, and a constant straining to pass urine, which is sometimes tinged with blood. Very often a cat which is perfectly clean in its habits will become suddenly dirty and refuse to use its tray; also it may cry out while straining. Town cats, usually through faulty feeding and lack of exercise, often fall victims to cystitis. As a rule, the trouble can be treated successfully, provided that you can get the vet in time. Keep the cat warm, and to prevent a recurrence persuade it to drink as much as possible. Adhere strictly to the vet's advice regarding diet, and give enough bicarbonate of potash to cover a threepenny piece mixed with the food or milk two or three times a day. When milk is given, it should always be warmed.

INFECTIOUS ENTERITIS   This is by far the most serious of all feline illnesses. It is extremely contagious and has a very high mortality rate: nearly three-quarters of the cases that occur prove fatal, death taking place within forty-eight hours. Symptoms are general listlessness and vomiting of mucous fluid, which within a few hours may change to a yellow or greenish froth. Sometimes diarrhœa is present, but not always. Usually there is an excessive thirst, and the kitten will sit over a bowl of water which it has not the strength to drink. Rapid wasting, cloudy eyes, ulceration of the mouth and tongue are further evidence of this terrible disease.

Call a vet immediately, for, to put it plainly, if you want to save your pet, there is no time to lose. In spite of continual scientific research, unfortunately, at the time of writing there is still no definite cure for infectious enteritis. Among treatments which do prove successful are sulpha drugs, penicillin, enterofagos,[1] and various homœopathic remedies, but because one cat recovers as the result of one of these treatments there is no guarantee that another will do so. In America there are various anti-feline enteritis serums, and most breeders in that country have their kittens vaccinated before offering them for sale. Even so, there is still no guarantee that the illness will not be contacted. Before the war Messrs. Burroughs Wellcome prepared a very effective vaccine both as a preventative and for inoculation in the early stages of the disease. No doubt this will be available again in the future.

One of the greatest difficulties in this and other serious

[1] A recently established medicine in ampoule form.

illnesses is to persuade the cat to take enough nourishment to fight the disease, although it is doubtful if any good can come of forcing food while the sickness is persistent. Most probably the vet will suggest glucose injections or something similar during the very early stages of the illness, but after a while some more natural attempt must be made to induce the cat to eat. Highly concentrated foods will be necessary, but they must also be those which are easily digested, and they must only be given in very tiny quantities at a time. Brand's Essence, beef-tea, egg and milk, or Benger's Food are all nourishing, and should be offered by dipping your finger in the liquid and then holding it gently to the cat's nose. It may lap the food from your finger; it may take no notice at all. Should the latter happen, the vet might suggest that you try feeding with a special spoon, inserting the spout very gently between the cat's side teeth and cheek, so that the mixture can be poured slowly into its mouth. The vet will advise you how often to feed the cat, but it will probably be at about hourly intervals, and will have to be kept up both day and night.

Although your pet must be kept warm during the illness, a stuffy atmosphere should be avoided. Any discharge from the eyes and nose should be wiped away gently with cotton-wool, and if the fur and rear parts become soiled from sickness or diarrhœa, these should be cleaned in the same manner. But try not to linger over all this longer than absolutely necessary. An ill cat likes to be left in peace, and too much handling may even delay recovery.

After a case of infectious enteritis, the greatest care must be taken to disinfect the premises thoroughly; also everything with which the cat has been in contact. Bedding should be burnt, feeding dishes destroyed, and baskets either replaced or scrubbed with very strong disinfectant.

Whether your pet recovers or not, keep away from cat shows for a time, and, indeed, from anywhere that cats are kept. It is now a well-known fact that enteritis germs can be carried on a person's clothes, shoes, and even in their letters. So do remember your friends' cats, and however badly you want another kitten, do not have one for at least *six* months.

Finally, do not assume from the foregoing paragraphs that your Siamese cat will necessarily be a victim of this disease. An epidemic may occur only once in a while. Nevertheless, every cat-owner should have a knowledge of the early symptoms of infectious enteritis, so that veterinary assistance may be called without delay.

FELINE DISTEMPER This is another terribly contagious illness among cats, and although in some cases the symptoms may appear rather like those of infectious enteritis, veterinary science has proved that the mortality rate is not nearly so high. Not that any cat suffering from distemper can afford to be neglected, but, given expert treatment and very careful nursing, a good recovery can usually be made.

While infectious enteritis usually attacks young kittens, distemper is inclined to be more dangerous to older cats. The disease occurs in various forms, but the more usual is a catarrhal illness which commences with much sneezing and a watery discharge from the eyes and nose. There may also be dribbling from the mouth. Soon this changes to a thick mucus, there is much fever, the eyes become inflamed, and the coat hard and staring. Owing to ulceration of the mouth and throat, great difficulty is experienced in swallowing. Sometimes there is sickness and diarrhœa; usually the breath is foul. Still further complications may be coughs and bronchitis, when the condition becomes very serious indeed.

For treatment, the vet will probably prescribe M. and B. or penicillin, but until he arrives you can safely give homœopathic aconite to keep the fever down. Follow the vet's directions very carefully, and be sure to keep the cat warm and out of draughts. Even if your pet appears to make a very quick recovery, do not let it out until the vet assures you it is safe to do so. Quite apart from the danger of infection to other cats in the neighbourhood, there is the very grave risk of a relapse. I have seen more than one cat made very ill indeed only through the thoughtlessness of its owner.

As in the case of infectious enteritis, the cat will probably refuse all food. The strength should be maintained either with thin barley water or water to which glucose has been added. Later you can build up your pet's resistance with more concentrated foods, as has already been described.

Discharge from the eyes and nose should be wiped gently with cotton-wool dipped in warm water, and the mouth should be swabbed out with a weak solution of Condy's Fluid and water or diluted T.C.P. If the eyelids are sore, as frequently happens, smear them very gently with just a touch of vaseline or golden eye ointment. A little glycerine rubbed on the nostrils will prevent soreness. For a mild laxative, give homœopathic nux vomica 3X.

After an attack of distemper, all bedding must be burnt and thorough disinfection of the premises carried out as described above.

93

9

The Place of the Siamese in the Cat Fancy

"THE Siamese is a splendid show cat, and is, moreover, of considerable value, and it will be doubtless one of the first rescued from the 'variety' class. I look forward to the Crystal Palace or any other comprehensive exhibition of cats taking the initiative and provide a separate class."

So wrote John Jennings in his book, *Domestic and Fancy Cats*, which was published over half a century ago, in 1893. Enthusiastic as Mr. Jennings was at that time, no doubt even he might have been surprised at the remarkable popularity of Siamese cats to-day. As recorded at the beginning of this book, more than 8,000 were registered with the Governing Council of the Cat Fancy in the three years following the war.

Why are Siamese cats in such demand? I put this question to several of our leading fanciers, requesting their various opinions as to the future of this favourite breed.

The first opinion comes from Mrs. Duncan Hindley, the distinguished judge and breeder, who admits to being in love with these cats ever since she brought her first Siamese home to England from Malaya in 1921. Since that time Mrs. Hindley has bred many champions, and her famous Prestwick prefix has become a household word among fanciers both in Britain and overseas.

This is what she says:

"I think the chief reasons for the tremendous popularity of Siamese cats are their very loving disposition and their faithfulness to their own master or mistress. To these I would add cleverness, character, and also beauty of colouring and shape. I think people will always want Siamese cats, although, of course, the demand may fluctuate owing to lack of money. Certainly the standard of Siamese cats did deteriorate during and after the war, partly owing to high prices, due to the big demand. Too many undesirable people started breeding to gain these high prices and not for the love of the cats or for love of good breeding. But the standard is now definitely improving."

To novice breeders, Mrs. Hindley would offer this advice:

"Start with only one or, at the most, two queens, and these should be the very best you can afford. Do *not* start with a stud cat until experience is gained with breeding. Stud work is the most difficult and responsible work and needs infinite patience. Patience, love of animals, and cleanliness are the chief attributes of a good breeder—also ability to handle cats well."

Questions in similar vein were put to Mrs. Elsie Hart. Mrs. Hart is a renowned judge, breeder of the famous Sealsleeve Siamese cats and Hon. Secretary of the Siamese Cat Club.

She considers that the chief reason for the popularity of Siamese cats is that they are different. "The owner of a Siamese never wants any other variety." Regarding the standard of the breed, Mrs. Hart feels that the Siamese exhibited at the first post-war shows were definitely inferior to those produced before the war, but the standard has improved considerably during the past year or so and is almost back to pre-war level.

Mrs. Hart has the following comments to make on the breeding of first-class specimens:

"Pedigree is the first and most important point to consider. The present-day winners are being bred from the same strains which bred winners in pre-war days. New strains built up from unknown parents are useless. A winning cat with questionable ancestors will usually not amount to much, but the cat with the pedigree behind it will throw good quality stock for generations after. This has been proved during the post-war shows."

And here are the views of Mr. B. A. Stirling-Webb, another eminent judge and fancier, and Hon. Treasurer of the Siamese Cat Club:

"To raise the standard of the Siamese the breeder must know what to aim at. It is not enough to study the official standard of points, for unless comparison with other cats is possible, one can easily be deluded into the belief that one's own is perfect. The way to know Siamese is to take every opportunity to see the best. Shows afford chances for this and for discovering what constitutes 'type'. Having arrived at a mental picture of perfection, one sees where one's own cat fails, and the task of choosing a stud for her is simplified. The aim should always be for improvement on the dam, and it is worth remembering that a cat which sires one champion may easily sire another and is therefore probably more suitable as a stud than the champion himself."

And, finally, an interesting opinion from Mrs. E. Towe, who, besides breeding Siamese and other cats with great success, finds time to act as Hon. Secretary to two of Britain's foremost cat clubs:

"I do not think the cats are as inbred now as they were a few years ago, as I think people have seen the dangers of such a policy before it is too late. Many breeders seem to believe in line breeding, which I also think is permissible occasionally if both cats are good."

Now let us consider just a few of the famous Siamese cats of to-day. To begin with, there is Champion Prestwick Penglima Pertama, a beautiful seal-pointed male whose perfect shape and eye colour have been described by a leading judge as "all one could wish for". This cat was bred by Mrs. Duncan Hindley and is the grandson of Champion Prestwick Pertama, which was considered by Mrs. Hindley to be her most successful cat of the past.

Mr. Stirling-Webb's Champion Chirmon Lon is an outstanding example of a female with really beautiful colouring, dense seal-points and wonderful blue eyes. Sired by Hoveton Emperor, a very famous cat of the past, this is yet another instance of what Mrs. Hart means when she says that pedigree is the first and most important point to consider. Chirmon Lon was the first seal-pointed Siamese to be awarded a full championship after the war.

Another lovely cat is Doneraile Debutante, bred by Mrs. K. R. Williams. Debutante is not only the holder of many awards herself, but has passed on her excellent qualities to her kittens. Her daughter, Diane, and litter brother were voted as best pair of kittens at the Siamese Cat Club's Show in 1948, while another daughter, Champion Doneraile Drusilla, has been voted best Siamese at many shows in the United States of America. Her grandson, Doneraile Dandie, attained his championship at the Washington Show at the age of eleven months. Mrs. Williams certainly has good reason to feel proud of her cats' record.

Mention has been made earlier in this book of Mrs. McGregor's seal-pointed Champion Inwood Shadow, acclaimed by judges as the best Siamese female seen in Britain since the war. Shadow was one of a lovely litter of six kittens, three males and three females, and this is what her owner has to say about her:

"Shadow was a little smaller than the rest and had rather difficulty in holding her own. Even when very small, she was outstanding even among that lovely litter. She went on improving, and I showed her as a kitten with her brother, Inwood Ching, but Ching always did better than she did. However, she went on improving, especially after having kittens, to which she was a wonderful mother. At last I managed to get her into perfect condition for showing, and in the season beginning with the Siamese Cat Club's Show in October 1949 she did wonderfully well, winning four championships, twenty-three firsts, and very many awards."

Another instance of how a kitten can improve beyond even the breeder's expectations is that of Champion Hillcross Song, owned by Mrs. Druce and bred by Mrs. Towe. Song was winner of the open male adult class at the Siamese Cat Club's Show in 1949. He is a most attractive cat with well-set ears on a long, wedge-shaped head, really beautiful eye colour, good coat, dense seal-points, and whip tail.

Mention must also be made of Mrs. Wridgway's Sapphire of Sabrina, a very well-known winner since 1947, when she was awarded second place in the Championship class at the age of nine months. The following year at the Siamese Cat Club's Show, she won her first Championship certificate, then again at Birmingham, her second Championship certificate. In little over two years this lovely cat won fifteen first prizes, nineteen second prizes, and two challenge certificates at championship shows, besides very many other awards at smaller shows all over the country.

Another Siamese with a very successful record is Mrs. Parker's Lindale Simon Pie, which leapt into fame at about five months old, when he was voted best exhibit at the Kensington Kitten Show in 1948 and best kitten at three successive London shows. Up to April 1950, Simon had won nineteen first prizes, six silver cups; also silver and bronze medals.

This cat has a very interesting story, for his mother had nine kittens, but was much too ill to feed them. The vet took her away to operate and suggested putting the kittens to sleep. "But", says Mrs. Parker, "I decided to try feeding them by hand." For the first two days they were fed almost every hour with a valve rubber on the end of an eye-dropper, and kept warm in the airing cupboard in a box deep with kapok. In this way Mrs. Parker managed to rear the five males successfully. They all fulfilled their early promise, but Simon's triumphs have won him an international reputation.

IO

Some Famous Owners

AMONG all our feline friends, it seems that the Siamese appeals most to artistic people. Go into the homes of actors, sculptors, musicians, and writers, and you will find that many of them enjoy the companionship of these beautiful and intelligent cats.

Compton Mackenzie, who, in his broadcasts and literature, has described the Siamese cat so perfectly, pays special tribute to its fidelity and love of people rather than of place. At one time this famous author kept no less than eleven Siamese cats. He has told how one of them, a cat called Pauline, would bring admirers home and offer them her dinner. Then, as soon as they had eaten it, she would turn on them with insults! Mr. Mackenzie's witty speeches, spiced with lively anecdotes, have been a feature of the Siamese Cat Club's Championship Show for many years.

Another great admirer of these cats is Vivien Leigh, the celebrated actress. When she was making the film of *Anna Karenina*, her devoted pet, New, was a frequent visitor to the studio. Were you to visit Miss Leigh in her dressing-room during this time it would not have surprised you to hear a loud "miaow" coming from the corner of the divan or hearthrug. Unfortunately, she no longer has New, but tells me that Boy, another Siamese cat, has taken his place.

Mention has already been made of Beverley Nichols' cats, One and Four. Mr. Nichols says that he is always annoyed when he hears people say that Siamese cats are exactly like dogs: "This is a superficial observation based on the fact that they can be trained to come for walks with one, and that they are sometimes more demonstrative. In all essential respects they are poles apart from dogs. They have an astonishing independence, which no dog has, and a superb sense of dignity—which is also lacking in dogs. As for their going for walks, etc., any cat who has been really well trained will do the same. I have one Siamese and one non-Siamese, and they follow me about all over the garden."

Mr. Nichols maintains that Siamese cats are extraordinarily sensitive, and can be made actually ill by unkindness or neglect. "I treat mine", he says, "not only with affection, but with *politeness*, and would not dream of pushing him out of a chair even if I wished to sit in it myself. Maybe that is going to extremes, but that is how I feel about it."

Michael Joseph is very well known among cat-lovers. Indeed, it would be most interesting to know quite how many people became infatuated with Siamese cats as a result of reading his delightful story, *Charles*. Here is but one description of this beloved pet:

"With me at all events Charles seemed to know he would not be misunderstood. When he stroked his back against my

XXXII. Clonlost Yo Yo with Fern, daughter of Mr. R. Warner of Sevenoaks, who owns this best exhibit at the 1949 Siamese Cat Club Championship Show, at Lime Grove Hall, Shepherd's Bush, London. This cat is now a champion.

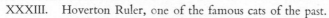

XXXIII.   Hoverton Ruler, one of the famous cats of the past.

XXXIV.   Mrs. Hindley's Prestwick Peggotty.

XXXV. Miss Dixon's champion, Pita.

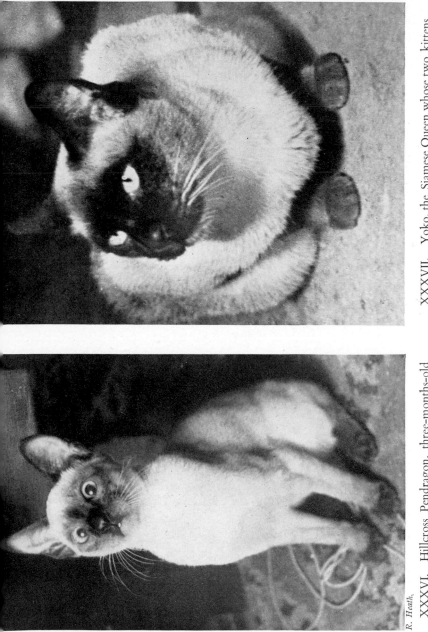

R. Heath,

XXXVI. Hillcross Pendragon, three-months-old kitten, bred by Mrs. Towe.

XXXVII. Yoko, the Siamese Queen whose two kittens are permanent passengers on the "Stratheden", travelling backwards and forwards to Australia. Owner of Yoko is Mrs. E. Pinder of Mundesley, Norfolk.

leg and turned round to do it on the other side, he knew
I would understand, and bend down to caress him or pick
him up. He loved to be picked up and held like a baby. He
was as much at ease on my shoulder as on the ground and
purred his continuous pleasure. Besides all these exhibitions
of his affection, he had one habit which in my experience of
cats is unique. As soon as I took off my shoes he would
transfer his attention to them, rubbing his head against each
shoe in turn, and even pushing the shoe along the ground
in his pleasure.

"From my dressing-room he would follow me to my bed,
which he regarded as partly his property. In cold weather
he liked to sleep under the eiderdown. He had a decided
preference for the middle of the bed and seemed not to mind
my feet. If he were still in a playful mood, he amused himself by trying to bite, or, rather, pretending to bite, my
feet through the blankets. He bore no malice if I accidentally
kicked him aside in the night, but that was no easy matter,
for he was a heavy cat. *J'y suis, j'y reste* was his motto, and
no matter how much I disturbed him, even to the point of
pushing him off the bed altogether, back he would come and
settle down again to sleep.

"He did not sleep regularly on my bed, sometimes preferring his open basket or a chair in one of the other rooms. He
seldom went out at night, although he had a mischievous
habit of asking to be let out an hour or so before bed-time.
This was usually in the summer, and on warm nights he
would take a delight in staying out until I had undressed.
He knew perfectly well that I would come down in my
dressing-gown, open the door and clap my hands—the

H   103

recognised signal for calling him in. Many a time—usually when the moon was full and went to his head—he pretended not to hear, and only when I had lost patience and had nearly roused the whole neighbourhood clapping my hands and shouting at him would he dash into the house, usually from a place of concealment a few yards away, where he had been laughing to himself all the time."

Olivia Manning, author of *The Remarkable Expedition*, *An Artist among the Missing*, and many other well-known books, has an adored Siamese cat called Eebou, and sends me this description of her:

"Eebou, when a very small kitten, would claim attention by sitting on the toe of one's shoe. With her white breast curving over the instep, she would stare steadily upward looking more like a baby owl than a cat. As no one can repeat the word 'owl' without discomfort, we decided to call her Hibou (Siam having once been a French possession) and the spelling we Siamesed into Eebou. Sometimes she has a wish for horse-meat, sometimes for whale, sometimes for tinned rabbit; she chooses to starve rather than eat one of these when preferring another. She sleeps with us in turns. Leaving my husband in the middle of the night, she will arrive on my pillow, point with her cold nose at the top of the covers, and, when I lift them for her, she will slide like silk into my arms and make the bed quiver with her purring.

"When she has been left for some time alone in the flat, she will welcome our return by throwing herself in ecstasy at our feet, lying as though comatose until picked up. If we come in with arms full of parcels so that she realises we cannot pick her up, she will follow us until the parcels are put down; then she will re-throw herself as much as to say, 'Now we can get on with things.' She has one chair that she has torn to ribbons; knowing our fear that she may start on another, she will pretend to tear at any new piece of furniture introduced into the flat. This is a joke, of course, and when we chase her off it is difficult not to hear the laughter that convulses her whole body. Preparations for visitors put her into a frenzy of excitement, so she goes round the flat like a racing-car; however, she tends to sulk when they arrive. She will retrieve a rabbit's paw, but not often; she will pretend to be a wild cat and, at a signal, race from one point to another, growling and taking spectacular leaps with ears flattened. At times when she has shown unreasonable jealousy, we have threatened to have her psychoanalysed, but she is less of an imaginative than of a scientific temperament. At the moment she is engaged on the problem of why water comes out of taps."

James and Pamela Mason, who need no introduction to cat-lovers, keep several Siamese. However, even the most ardent admirer of these cats will admit how difficult they can be until they settle down with a new owner. In *Cats in Our Lives* (Michael Joseph Ltd.), Pamela Mason has amusingly described how her first Siamese cat reacted to her overtures of friendship:

"As a wedding present, I was given my first Siamese. I had never seen one before; hardly heard of them even. My friend, Ilena Silver, bought him for me and delivered him the night before the wedding. He was about ten weeks old, very loud-mouthed. Instead of taking to me immediately like every cat I had met in the past, he rushed under the bed and made terrible, threatening noises. No amount of coaxing had any effect. I couldn't sit up all night, because I wanted to look reasonably fresh for my wedding, so I got into bed and managed to get a little sleep when the noises temporarily subsided. But at about four in the morning I was awakened by the most fearful yowls, and any Siamese cat lover will know what I mean. When a Siamese really gives voice it is something: a mixture of a baby's scream, howling wind, and the death agony of a soprano. (I have learned to love the sound.)

"Anyhow, my new kitten was lying on his back under my bed with all his claws stuck into the mattress and dragging himself around under the bed, letting out these fearful yells. I got out of bed and lay on the floor, trying to quieten him. My pleas were quite useless. He struck out at me and hissed and told me to go to hell. I had never been treated in this way by a cat before. I loved all cats and all cats loved me, I thought. But there was no getting round this new situation. The kitten expressed his feelings with perfect clarity. When I offered food, he spat and shouted. When I tried to stroke him, he scratched.

"Finally, I told him that I hated him and all Siamese cats. I couldn't understand him at all. I decided that in the morning I would tell Ilena that she must take him back, because he was a wild, uncontrollable, mean little animal.

"This was Gamma, my first Siamese cat. I have never been without one since and I never will be. Let all the praise that has ever been heaped on dogs, horses, cats, and children be added together in favour of this wonderful friend."

And, finally, here is a very interesting and amusing story

from the well-known author, Pamela Wynne. It is about one of her own cats and she calls him "Naughty Shorty": "Shorty is a seal-pointed Siamese cat. He is one of a family of four cats: two blue-pointed Siamese and a coal black cross-breed: the result of a rather disgraceful incident in the life of one of the blue-points. But all are equally beloved; and fortunately they all get on extremely well together. But outside the home circle Shorty is inclined to be pugnacious; and he is not altogether beloved by the owners of other cats. He should not be pugnacious; he has no reason to be; but the fact remains that he is. So eventually he has come to be known as Naughty Shorty. This is a mistake, because if you designate a cat as naughty, he will become more naughty. Shorty has become more naughty as you will soon see.

"One day, as I stood gazing out of the window, I saw Shorty crossing the lawn with a live chicken in his mouth. Not a grown-up chicken; a tiny one. Where had he got it from? I was horrified: chickens are valuable things, apart from any cruelty. Knowing that if I attempted to get hold of him he would bolt, I remained where I was. What was he going to do with it?

"He obviously had his plan all mapped out. There is a large cat run in my garden, the access to which is through a little wire gate. Shorty had reached the gate, and with infinite care was manoeuvring himself and the chicken through it. Once in the run he let the chicken go, and then folded his paws and crouched down to watch it. It was unhurt . . . a little unsteady on its feet, but it tumbled about for a minute or two and then, recovering its equilibrium, it stood on tiptoe and flapped its tiny wings. Shorty appeared pleased; and, seeing that he did not seem to be going to attack it, I went downstairs and out into the garden. Naughty Shorty!

"But Shorty only glanced up at me with contempt and went on looking at the chicken, so rather feebly I decided that I couldn't do anything except feed the chicken and rig it up a cosy little nest in the cat-house, and hope for the best.

"And this I did. But the next day, when exactly the same thing happened again, I became very much perturbed. Where were the chickens coming from? Everybody I knew who kept chickens kept them shut up. Chickens nowadays are valuable things; somebody must be very much upset at their disappearance. And yet, if I broadcast what was happening, some ill-disposed person—and there are persons ill-disposed towards cats, although it is a thing very difficult to believe—some ill-disposed person might either shoot or damage Shorty.

"And what was the result? The result was that one of the cat runs has now been turned into a fowl run in which disport themselves seven extremely robust buff orpington chickens; sex jealousy, owing to his own disabilities, had evidently prevented Shorty from bringing home a rooster! And now eggs will soon be arriving. Naughty Shorty? Well, it will be rather difficult to keep that up when, instead of something prehistoric from Poland, I sit down to an egg that will remind me of the old days. Besides, in the face of such complacency, it is difficult to remain shocked. For Shorty now spends most of his time spread out on the wire ceiling of the erstwhile cat run, gazing down at his hostages. Naughty Shorty? Well, you may call him that if you like, but I'm not going to!"

11

Siamese Cats in Other Lands

ALTHOUGH in some countries Siamese cats do not yet enjoy the same tremendous popularity as in Britain, they are gaining favour everywhere. This especially applies to the U.S.A. and Canada. The United States has its own Siamese Cat Society which organises special shows in conjunction with all breed exhibits sponsored by the American Cat Association and the Cat Fanciers' Federation, which are two of the four registering bodies in that country.

Cat shows in the U.S.A. are very gay and colourful affairs. Many more shows are held than in Britain, and fanciers have a far greater opportunity of exhibiting their stock. So enthusiastic are the American breeders that they are prepared to travel great distances to the shows, often by air. It is permissible—indeed, customary—to decorate the show pens in as elaborate a fashion as the exhibitor pleases, and often there is a prize for the best decorated cage. Cats are to be seen reclining in wicker baskets or sleeping peacefully on silk-embroidered cushions, their previous winning rosettes and ribbons attached to the respective pens.

All the foremost breeders in the U.S.A. import cats from Britain, for they know that a well-bred British cat will undoubtedly be a great asset to their own stock. Mention has already been made in a previous chapter of Champion Doneraile Drusilla, bred by Mrs. K. R. Williams of Surrey. Drusilla was sent to Mr. and Mrs. Sven Nelson of Braintree, Mass., and besides achieving championship status herself, this cat has passed on her fine qualities to her offspring, H.R.H. of Ebon Mask, also owned by Mr. and Mrs. Sven Nelson.

Another famous cat from Britain is seal-pointed Lemling English Rose, bred by Mrs. Ella B. Martin of Chelmsford, and now owned by Mr. Price Cross of Dallas, Texas. Rose was the only female in a litter of eight kittens and was sired by Mrs. Duncan Hindley's celebrated stud, Champion Prestwick Penglima Pertama, which has also been alluded to earlier in this book.

When Mr. B. A. Stirling-Webb was invited to judge the National Siamese Cat Club Speciality Show in New York, December 1949, he reported that blue-points at this show were superior to ours in the matter of colour, "their points being a definite blue shade rather than the grey tone which seems to prevail over here". Mr. Stirling-Webb gave the award of best blue-point in the show to Kaybee Mia Lescula, yet another British-bred cat, this time by Miss Kennedy Bell of Highgate, North London.

Fall

XXXIX.   Mrs. Macdonald's Holtwood Morning Dew.

Fall

XXXVIII.   Mrs. F. Macdonald's Raard Glima and Raard
Soo–San.

XL.   Doneraile Debutante (*right*) and Doneraile Diane. Breeder Mrs. K. R. Williams.

Here is the official standard of points and descriptions as issued by the Siamese Cat Society of America, Inc. It is very interesting to compare this with our own scale of points given on pp. 8–9.

SEAL-POINT

SCALE

BODY COLOUR 15
Even pale fawn or cream, slightly darker across the shoulders, shading gradually into a lighter colour on the stomach and chest. The coat to be a warm fawn with no grey. In judging body colour in older cats, allowance should be made for a darker coat, as Siamese darken with age, but the body should not be so dark as to eliminate contrast with the points. Kittens lighter in colour.

POINTS 15
Mask, ears, legs, feet and tail dense and clearly defined, all of the *same* shade of deep seal brown. Mask should be connected by tracings with the ears, except in kittens.

SHAPE, BODY AND TAIL 20
The body should be medium in size, dainty, long, and svelte. Neck long and slender, legs proportionately slim, hind legs slightly higher than front, feet small and oval in shape. Tail long and tapering to a fine point. A slight kink in the end is allowed. Winners to be withheld from bobbed, screwed, badly kinked, or pompon tails.

III

HEAD AND EARS 15
The head should be long and taper in straight lines from the ears to a narrow muzzle, with no break at the whiskers. Skull to be flat and the nose to be a continuation of the forehead with no break. In profile, a straight line is seen from the centre of forehead to tip of nose. Allowance to be made for jowls in the stud cat. Ears erect, rather large, pricked, and wide at base.

EYES (COLOUR AND SHAPE) 20
Eyes, clear and of a vivid deep blue colour. Eye aperture almond in shape and slanting towards the nose in true Oriental fashion. Preferably not crossed.

COAT 10
Short, fine in texture and lying close to the body.

CONDITION 5
Perfect physical conditon. Not fat, inclined to muscle.

TOTAL 100

BLUE-POINT

The above standard to apply to the blue-point Siamese, except the coat is to be a silvery blue, slightly darker across the shoulders, changing gradually to an oyster white on the stomach and chest. Points to be of a much darker blue, but of the same tone as the coat. There must be no warm tone of fawn in the coat. Allowance made for older cats. Kittens lighter in colour.

UNDESIRABLE
Round-headed, fat, thick-set specimens, apparent
hood, rough or shaggy coats, odd eye colour,
grey or yellowish tinge in eyes. Tabby or ticked
markings, light hairs appearing in points. White
feet or toes. Receding chin.

Siamese predominate in the South African Cat Fancy,
although a great number of them are hybrid. Many of these
specimens are black-coated, with blue eyes typical of the
breed. At a show held by the Western Province Cat Club,
Siamese prevailed over the other exhibits to the extent of
thirty-one out of a total of fifty-four. The prize for the best
exhibit in the show was awarded to Momchao Phaun, a cat
actually bred by the King of Siam himself and owned by
Mrs. Bendyshe Walton of Grahamstown. Another winner
was the Siamese kitten, Sebastian Periwinkle of Brakkekloof,
owned by Miss F. Pocock, Chairman of the South African
Cat Union.

Owing to the beautiful climate in South Africa, shows are
usually held in the open air. Cats are not penned as in
Britain and the U.S.A., but sit in collar and lead and watch
the proceedings, or in the arms of their owners. Here is an
extract from South African show rules: "Every exhibit
should have a comfortable basket, car, or lap in which to sit
during the show and be seen by the public. The owner
must accompany the exhibit and be in the judging room
during the judging for the class entered, and must carry the
exhibit to the judges' table when required."

The Siamese Fancy in Australia is not as yet of any

considerable size, but interest is rapidly increasing. Special enthusiasm appears to be shown for seal-pointed cats; the blue-pointed variety are at present almost unknown. However, one or two ardent breeders are importing them from Britain. At a show held in Melbourne, twelve Siamese cats were exhibited, and created so much interest that enthusiasts decided to organise a special club for the breed, with the result that the Siamese Cat Club of Australia was born. This club models its rules as closely as possible on the British Siamese Cat Club, and it works to raise the standards of Siamese cats in its own country.

On the Continent, Siamese cats are very popular indeed, although at present the standard is not considered to be as high as in Britain. Short, kinked tails appear to be a special feature, and in describing one of the exhibits for her report of the Cat Club de Paris Show in 1949, our own eminent judge, Mrs. Joan Thompson, wrote: "This fault I found in nearly every exhibit, and some of the tails brought memories of the Siamese as they were in England when I first commenced to handle them as a steward over twenty years ago."

And, again, in reporting on the International Cat Show at San Pellegrino, July 1948, Marcel Reney has written: "In Siamese the males were better than the females, but the heads were too round, and the colour too dark; several had beautiful blue eyes. They bear out what I have written in my book, *Nos amis les Chats*, that the exhibitors on the Continent should import several good specimens from England to get back the standard of the beautiful Siamese."

Nevertheless, in all fairness, it must be said that Mrs.

Thompson also praised several of the exhibits at the Cat Club de Paris Show most highly, and was particularly complimentary about two chocolate-pointed specimens, one of which she awarded special prize for the best Siamese.

As in the U.S.A., Continental shows are very gay occasions, usually lasting for two days or more. As a rule, judging takes place on the first day, and the general public are admitted on the second and third days to view the exhibits. Doors are not closed until 9 or 10 p.m. each evening.

12

To Sum Up

COLLARS

GENERALLY speaking, there is no need for a cat to wear a collar. However, opinions do vary upon this matter, especially among Siamese-owners, who often like to adorn their pets in this way. Certainly the Siamese cat looks very attractive with a collar, but the ordinary leather type is dangerous, because the natural instinct of the cat to climb trees and fences involves the risk of strangulation on branches and so on.

Cæsar never wears a collar excepting when I have to take him on a journey, or if he is to stay with strangers. He then wears a special accident-proof collar, which is made of elastic and recommended by the animal welfare societies. In such circumstances this type of collar, with your pet's name and address on it, is a wise precaution, just in case the cat should get lost. A self-fitting harness and 60-in. lead, all in one, is also on the market. Made of strong, washable double elastic, this gives the cat complete freedom of movement and looks exceptionally smart on the Siamese.

MOVING HOUSE

Provided their owners are with them, most Siamese cats settle down quite easily in new surroundings. Nevertheless, home does mean a great deal to any cat, and the sight of removal men, boxes being packed, and so on is often very disturbing. If possible, ask a friend or neighbour to look after your pet while all these preparations are going on, but, of course, it must be someone whom the cat knows and likes, or it may not stay. When everything is ready, collect the cat and take it to the new home *yourself*. Naturally, this is an occasion when it should wear a collar.

If possible, have one room completely furnished by the time you arrive, so that the cat can be shut in there away from noises and strange men. Let this room contain all your pet's own personal belongings, such as baskets, blanket, feeding dishes, and so on. It is these little possessions that help the cat to settle down, so until it gets used to the new home never throw any of them away, however badly they may need replacing.

So far I have not actually had a permanent move with Cæsar, but I have taken him to new surroundings on holiday several times and have never had to confine him in any way. All the same, it might be safer not to let your pet into the new garden for a day or two. Let him explore the house as soon as the removal men have taken their departure, for he won't be happy until he has been on this voyage of exploration.

When moving to a new home, many people advise buttering a cat's paws, and certainly this is no idle superstition. The object is to keep puss busy with his toilet and so prevent him fretting. Should your Siamese disappear in spite of all these precautions, get in touch with the neighbours near your old address at once and ask them to let you know immediately if they should see the cat. Also, before moving, it would be wise to leave your new address with the police station and local tradesmen. Then, should any cat resembling yours appear, they will be able to contact you immediately. Do not be afraid of giving trouble; most people are only too pleased to help regarding pets. This was proved to me only recently, when one morning the baker appeared, long after his round was finished, to tell me that my cat was in a field about half a mile away, and did I think he would find his way home? I pointed to the kitchen, where through the open door Cæsar could be seen busily eating his dinner. The man could not understand it, for, as he said, the cat could not have walked faster than his van. On enquiry, we found that he had seen quite a different cat, but, not knowing many Siamese, he thought the wanderer must have been my Cæsar.

GOING ON HOLIDAY

Siamese are very accommodating and usually like to travel with their owners, so holidays should present no difficulties. Whenever possible, do take your pet with you; he (or she) will settle down quite quickly and the change of air will do him good.

There may be times, however, when it is difficult to take

Fall

XLI.   Mrs. Price's Devoran Donald.

Fall

XLII. Mrs. Price's Devoran Hermione.

XLIII. Mrs. Elsie Hart's famous cat Sealsleeve Shah-Pashah, founder of the Sealsleeve Strain.

XLIV.   Sally and Simon, owned by Mrs. Gotz of London.

a cat, and the problem will arise as to what you can do with it. If, during your absence, you can arrange for someone the cat knows to stay in your house and feed and care for it, this is always a good idea. Sometimes a neighbour can be asked to look after your pet, and as long as your Siamese likes him (or her), then this is also a good plan. But whoever is responsible should have the necessary leisure to spend a little time with the cat in addition to feeding it. This is most important, because Siamese cats do fret very badly if left for too long on their own. If you do not know anyone with whom you can safely leave your pet, then the only alternative is to board it out.

There are boarding kennels all over the country, some of which are as excellent as the others are unreliable. Advertisements are sometimes misleading, and personally I would never leave a pet anywhere without making thorough investigations first. Any boarding establishment that welcomes inspection without making a previous appointment may be regarded favourably. But this is not to say that you can take the cat along without making proper arrangements in advance. Realising the danger of infectious disease when too many cats are congregated together, reputable owners of boarding establishments will only take a limited number of visitors at a time. This usually necessitates fairly long-term planning.

While it is a little difficult to offer advice on this subject, I do feel most strongly that Siamese cats should only be left with people who really understand them. Naturally, a cat cannot be allowed complete freedom while in the charge of strangers. Nevertheless, an animal that has always been accustomed to liberty will not be happy if confined to one room, however large and comfortable the room may be and however well the cat is cared for otherwise. On the other hand, a pet which has been used to flat life will probably settle down better in such surroundings than in an outside cat house with a spacious run for exercise.

So far I have not needed to board my cat out, but should the occasion arise I feel I could leave him safely with any one of the following:

Dr. and Mrs. R. H. Francis, Low Knapp, Halstock, nr. Yeovil, Somerset. Only Siamese and their "stable companions" are taken, and no cat is accepted without owner's certificate of freedom from infection. Fuller particulars on application.

Mrs. W. M. Chapman, Blue House, Pot Kiln Chase, Gestingthorpe, Halstead, Essex.

Miss G. T. Allen, The Old Thatched Cottage, Rowtown, Addlestone.

Barkham Ridge Kennels, Nine Mile Ride, Finchampstead, Berks.

All the above are very highly recommended, and I understand that the cats are looked after with the same love and kindness as they receive at home.

CATS IN FLATS

There can be very little doubt that cats thrive best when given complete freedom. At the same time, it must be admitted that a great number of people do keep cats quite satisfactorily in flats, and, probably owing to its companionable qualities, the Siamese seems to be particularly favoured by flat-dwellers. Of course, any cat reared in this way must have as much sunshine as possible, and also regular exercise. One friend of mine has overcome the first difficulty by means of a large wire cage. This is made so that it exactly fits the open window. Screws are placed so that the window cannot open further than the top of the cage, thus assuring safety. I am told that the cat often sits there all day long, enjoying the fresh air and sunshine.

Regarding exercise, it is a perfectly simple matter to train Siamese cats to walk on a lead. They should also be encouraged to take some indoor exercise, and, as most of them are always ready for a game, this should not be difficult.

CATS AND DOGS

As a rule, Siamese cats get on very well with dogs, but unless the animals have been brought up together some form of careful introduction may be needed. During the very early days of the acquaintanceship, it is always a good idea to give slightly more attention to the pet that shared your household first. If it was the cat which was accustomed to receiving all your affection, then this is even more important, for Siamese cats are very jealous indeed.

Some people advocate having a cat's claws cut right down before introducing it to a new dog, and certainly the claws of a Siamese could be very dangerous if it should decide to attack. My own cat would never dream of being so wicked, so I have never needed to resort to this experiment. If you decide to try it, then leave the claw-cutting to a vet.

Another suggestion is to keep both animals in separate rooms for a few days so that they can smell each other's presence. This method is said to ensure a peaceful meeting. In my own experience, there is bound to be a short interval of sulking on the part of a full-grown cat before it settles down happily with a dog. One cat of mine disappeared for several days when I first brought a puppy home. She would return from time to time, but refuse to enter the house, just sitting at the window and spitting loudly at the dog inside. However, with patience, both animals were soon the best of friends. This particular cat, a non-Siamese and a terrible thief, would jump up on the table and pick out the choicest tit-bits, which she would throw to the puppy below. When the dog was older, it would also help its feline friend to wash her kittens!

EXPORTING SIAMESE CATS

British-bred cats have been held in high esteem for many years, and are now breaking records in the export market. Particularly great is the demand from the U.S.A., but tremendous enthusiasm has also been created in Canada and many other countries.

Air-travel is favoured by nearly all our leading breeders as the quickest and most convenient way of sending cats abroad. Two veterinary certificates of health are necessary before any cat can go overseas. There are at present a number of currency regulations in force, and new breeders intending to export their stock should satisfy themselves on this point before dispatching. Enquiries in the first place should be made through the livestock department of one of the leading transport companies, when every help will be given.

Naturally, it is essential to export only the finest of Britain's cats, and to ensure doing this it is suggested that the opinion of an established judge is always asked before deciding to send any stock abroad. In this way, Britain will continue to maintain the goodwill and very high esteem of fanciers overseas.

THE CATS' PROTECTION LEAGUE

Mention has already been made of some of the services which Siamese cat owners can obtain through the Cats' Protection League.

Since its foundation in 1927, this splendid society has helped many hundreds of our feline friends and been of tremendous assistance to cat-lovers both in Britain and overseas. The Cats' Protection League, with headquarters at Slough, Buckinghamshire, is the only organisation of its kind which devotes itself entirely to the welfare of cats and kittens. Indeed, its wide distribution of educational literature has initiated hundreds of people who might never have become cat-conscious otherwise.

Clinical work, which is mainly carried out at Headquarters, ranges from major operations performed by the League's veterinary surgeon, to treatment such as teeth-scaling, ear-cleaning, and so on. In addition to this, every year, homes are found for hundreds of otherwise unwanted kittens, and many lost cats are restored safely to their owners.

This rescue and clinical work is catered for under the League's special "Tailwavers" scheme, through which our own "pet" cats are able to help their less fortunate fellows, the "strays". On enrolment each cat is given a number. All you need to do is send the name and age of your pet, giving the date of birth if possible and any other particulars you care to add. "Tailwaver" donation is 5s. a year per cat, but where a member has several pets and cannot afford this amount, then all can be enrolled for such nominal fee as can be spared.

Besides the provision of grass seed and sexing charts, which I have mentioned earlier in this book, the Cats' Protection League also loans travelling baskets to subscribers, and there is an excellent library service. In addition, it issues a comprehensive monthly magazine, *The Cat*. Fuller details of membership will gladly be supplied by the League's Secretary, Mr. Albert A. Steward, on application to him at Prestbury Lodge, 29 Church Street, Slough, Bucks.

PERIODICALS FOR CAT-LOVERS

SIAMESE CAT CLUB NEWS SHEET. *Three times a year*. 5s. a year.

FUR AND FEATHER (official organ of the Governing Council of the Cat Fancy). *Weekly*. 4d. Watmoughs Ltd., Idle, Bradford, Yorks.

THE CAT FANCY. *Monthly*. 10d. per copy, or 10s. a year. The Loft, 18 South End, Kensington, London, W.8.

THE CAT (official organ of the Cats' Protection League). *Ten issues a year*. 5s. a year. 29 Church Street, Slough, Bucks.

OUR CATS. *Monthly*. 1s. 6d. 4 Carlton Mansions, Clapham Road, London, S.W.9.

CATS AND KITTENS. *Monthly*. 1s. 14, Queen Street, Derby.

CATS MAGAZINE (U.S.A.). *Monthly*. $3. 4 Smithfield Street, Pittsburgh 22, Pa., U.S.A.

Index